KEY ACCOUNT MANAGEMENT EXCELLENCE IN PHARMA & MEDTECH

Key Account Management Excellence in Pharma & Medtech is designed to help life sciences practitioners develop and execute innovative and effective key account management (KAM) strategies and capabilities. Pharmaceutical and medtech companies are increasingly pursuing KAM in response to the rapid rise of large, sophisticated and complex healthcare provider and payer systems and groups. Those that invest the time to get KAM right will protect their business and grow with these rising customers.

This book is groundbreaking in both its scope and its tailoring of leading KAM practices specifically for life sciences. The central theme is that "key account management is an organization-wide business strategy, not just a role or a sales-specific initiative." KAM is a strategy focused on providing unique offerings and value through an orchestrated, cross-functional, go-to-market model designed specifically to address the needs and engagement preferences of a unique segment of customers. The insights and practices shared in this book are designed to be a valuable reference at every stage of the KAM journey.

The book has been designed to facilitate a common language and deep understanding of KAM issues and leading practices organization-wide—particularly for life sciences executives, account managers and cross-functional team members responsible for building, transforming and supporting their organization's KAM strategies and capabilities.

MIKE MOORMAN is a Principal at ZS and leads the firm's key account management practice. Mike founded ZS's B2B commercial strategy and transformation practice and is a recognized expert in his field. He has worked globally and with more than 50 B2B organizations across 12 industries. Mike serves on the Board of Directors and the Research Advisory Board for the Strategic Account Management Association, and is an Adjunct Lecturer on Sales Strategy at Northwestern's Kellogg Executive Program. Mike has authored more than 60 publications and has been cited in leading publications including *Harvard Business Review*, *Financial Times*, *The Wall Street Journal*, *IndustryWeek*, *USA Today* and *Selling Power*.

"A truly holistic approach to KAM—one that the pharma and medtech industries desperately need."

Mitch Payne, *Global Head, Value and Access Excellence at Novartis Oncology*

"Pharma and medtech finally get their own KAM/SAM 'bible' with unique and relevant insights."

Dino Bertani, *Executive Director, International Strategic Account Management at AbbVie*

"A 'KAM blueprint must' for life sciences leaders at the critical juncture of shaping versus reacting to their future."

Barbara Ruhland, *Head of Strategic Accounts & Channel Management, US Radiology at Bayer*

"This thought leadership has been an invaluable playbook that I have read and reread to guide our progress."

Todd Burgess, *Global Key Account Manager Capabilities Leader at Merck*

"A terrific resource for SAM leaders in any industry—one I wish I had during my time at Schneider Electric."

Harvey Dunham, *Managing Director, Strategy and Marketing at Strategic Account Management Association*

"One of the most comprehensive books to date on the topic of SAM ... it uniquely addresses SAM in life sciences ... I believe this book should be a 'must-read' for any life sciences leader, account manager or cross-functional team member responsible for supporting SAM strategies and capabilities."

Denise Freier, *President and CEO, Strategic Account Management Association*

KEY ACCOUNT MANAGEMENT EXCELLENCE IN PHARMA & MEDTECH

Edited by Mike Moorman

Routledge
Taylor & Francis Group
LONDON AND NEW YORK

Cover image: ridvan_celik

First published 2022
by Routledge
4 Park Square, Milton Park, Abingdon, Oxon OX14 4RN

and by Routledge
605 Third Avenue, New York, NY 10158

Routledge is an imprint of the Taylor & Francis Group, an informa business

British Library Cataloguing-in-Publication Data
A catalogue record for this book is available from the British Library

Library of Congress Cataloging-in-Publication Data
Names: Moorman, Mike, editor.
Title: Key account management excellence in pharma & medtech / edited by Mike Moorman.
Description: New York, NY: Routledge, 2022. | Includes bibliographical references and index.
Identifiers: LCCN 2021052410 (print) | LCCN 2021052411 (ebook) |
ISBN 9781032128573 (hardback) | ISBN 9781032128580 (paperback) |
ISBN 9781003226512 (ebook)
Subjects: LCSH: Pharmaceutical industry—Management. | Medical supplies industry. | Marketing—Key accounts. | Customer services.
Classification: LCC HD9665.5 .K48 2022 (print) |
LCC HD9665.5 (ebook) | DDC 338.4/76151—dc23/eng/20211220
LC record available at https://lccn.loc.gov/2021052410
LC ebook record available at https://lccn.loc.gov/2021052411

ISBN: 978-1-032-12857-3 (hbk)
ISBN: 978-1-032-12858-0 (pbk)
ISBN: 978-1-003-22651-2 (ebk)

DOI: 10.4324/9781003226512

Typeset in Arial
by codeMantra

To Andy Zoltners, for inspiring us to think beyond

CONTENTS

FIGURES AND TABLES

FIGURES

TABLES

FOREWORD—A MESSAGE FROM THE CEO OF SAMA

As the CEO of the Strategic Account Management Association (SAMA), I'm pleased to share a few perspectives on strategic account management (SAM), often referred to as key account management (KAM), and the timely launch of this important book. With more than 18,000 members, SAMA is the world's largest and most diverse community of practitioners, academics, consultants and trainers dedicated to the advancement of SAM. Our extensive community provides unique insight on the leading SAM practices and trends, and one thing is clear: SAM has been and continues to be a critical priority for many, if not most, B2B and B2B2C organizations. SAM is a powerful and proven way to achieve unique value and impact with a company's most important customers, leading to deeper partnerships and greater success for both organizations. In a world characterized by hyper-competition, core product commoditization, uncertainty and increasingly demanding and sophisticated buyers, SAM is more important than ever.

Nowhere is this truer than in the life sciences industry. The rapid rise of large and sophisticated provider and payer systems has shifted control away from individual physicians to a more complex network of decision makers. It's interesting to note that just 10 years ago, only a handful of pharmaceutical and medtech companies were actively engaged with SAMA. Today, pharmaceutical and medtech corporate membership at SAMA has grown to the point where life sciences now represents one of the largest industry verticals within the SAMA community. This speaks volumes about the growing importance of SAM in life sciences.

I have no doubt that life sciences practitioners can and do benefit from insights and leading practices developed by SAM pioneers in other industries—as well as from best practices developed from within the life sciences industry itself. But one thing we have come to recognize at SAMA is that the challenges facing life sciences companies are unique. The decision dynamics in healthcare along with legal and regulatory considerations often require life-sciences-specific approaches to SAM. And much of life sciences is starting from commercial models geared toward individual physicians and surgeons, not complex networks of decision makers with broader needs and priorities. An intimate appreciation of these dynamics is essential for any organization seeking to apply and adapt SAM leading practices in life sciences.

This is why I'm so excited about *Key Account Management Excellence in Pharma & Medtech*, which is special in two important ways. First, it's one of the most comprehensive books to date on the topic of SAM. Second, it uniquely addresses SAM in life sciences. I'm proud that one of SAMA's long-standing board members, Mike Moorman, played a central role in developing and executing this book. Mike is a leading authority on SAM and one of the earliest proponents of approaching SAM "as an organization-wide business strategy, not as a role." In fact, he coined this positioning.

If you look at the backgrounds of the more than one dozen authors whom Mike brought together to write this book, you'll recognize what an undertaking it has been. The insights and leading practices shared in this book reflect a unique combination of cross-industry, issue and life sciences expertise. This trifecta required a village of cross-functional experts working together closely, which is a perfect illustration of SAM as an organization-wide business strategy.

A number of SAMA's staff and corporate members have had the opportunity to preview many sections of this book. The feedback has been outstanding. I believe this book should be a "must read" for any life sciences leader, account manager or cross-functional team member responsible for supporting SAM strategies and capabilities. At the same time, I also believe the concepts shared in this book apply broadly and will benefit anyone leading or supporting a SAM initiative, regardless of industry.

I'm sure that you'll find the insights in this book to be beneficial and inspiring, and I look forward to seeing you at one of SAMA's many upcoming events.

Sincerely,

Denise Freier
President and CEO
Strategic Account Management Association
200 W Madison, Suite 1040
Chicago, IL 60606
www.strategicaccounts.org

PREFACE—IMPORTANT INFORMATION ABOUT THIS BOOK

Mike Moorman

The recent and rapid rise of "organized customers"—large, sophisticated and complex healthcare provider and payer systems and groups—is proving to be a game-changer for life sciences companies. The influence and control these customers now exert over individual physician prescribing and surgeon product choice, as well as life sciences company access, is undeniable. And these trends are projected to intensify. Industry consolidation and business model evolution will continue as organized customers seek more effective ways to address the challenging mix of clinical, financial and experience objectives that define their mission.

The significant attention that pharmaceutical and medtech companies are now placing on key account management (KAM) is in direct response to these pivotal changes in the customer landscape. While the industry's traditional brand-centric and doctor-focused one-to-one selling models will continue to be important, these approaches don't meet the needs or engagement preferences of organized customers. Innovative approaches to KAM will be necessary to engage effectively with the broad network of decision makers within organized customers and to protect and deepen relationships within this increasingly dominant customer segment.

The vast majority of pharmaceutical and medtech companies have begun to pursue KAM, many in just the past few years. And while there are many bright spots and accomplishments, the industry is still at the early stages of this journey. Leading practices developed by KAM pioneers in other industries will be important for life sciences to understand. But many of those practices won't be simply "plug-and-play." For instance, legal and regulatory considerations within healthcare significantly impact the types of interactions and value exchange that can occur between manufacturers and healthcare providers. Furthermore, the gap between KAM and the deeply entrenched commercial models that currently exist within many life sciences companies is far greater than has been the case in many other industries. Pharmaceutical and medtech companies can and should learn from other industries, but they must also innovate KAM approaches in ways that address the unique dynamics in life sciences.

The primary motivation behind this book is to help life sciences practitioners achieve this objective. *Key Account Management Excellence in Pharma & Medtech* is groundbreaking in both its scope and its tailoring of leading KAM practices specifically for life sciences. The partnership of more than one dozen authors was necessary to bring together the depth and breadth of cross-industry, life sciences and functional expertise necessary to develop this book. In many ways, that coalition mirrors the cross-functional alignment and teamwork necessary for any organization to truly succeed at KAM.

The central theme of this book is that "key account management is an organization-wide business strategy, not just a role or a sales-specific initiative." If you only take away one thing from this book, we hope it will be this theme. KAM is about defining, tailoring and delivering a unique value strategy through a unique go-to-market model to an especially important and unique set of customers. KAM is dramatically different from the traditional brand-centric and doctor-focused strategies employed in life sciences and requires new ways of working and new capabilities organizationwide.

Our intended audience for *Key Account Management Excellence in Pharma & Medtech* is life sciences leaders, account managers and cross-functional team members responsible for building, transforming and supporting their organization's KAM strategies and capabilities. Cross-functional team members include marketing, sales, medical, analytics, technology and legal and regulatory functions. And while this book was written through the lens of life sciences, it's a beneficial resource for practitioners in any industry. The fundamental concepts we share derive from cross-industry leading practices and easily translate back.

The origin of this book is a structured series of white papers we recently developed titled "Achieving KAM excellence in life sciences." The overwhelmingly positive feedback and demand we received from early readers led us to expand the series in the form of this comprehensive publication. You should recognize that each chapter in this book was written as a stand-alone and independent paper, some of which are an updated version of the original white paper and others of which are exclusive to this book.

The chapters in this book largely follow our comprehensive KAM360™ framework that's introduced in Chapter 1, "KAM is a business strategy, not a role." The KAM360™ framework introduces 16 strategy and cross-functional capabilities that are the "drivers" of KAM effectiveness. Some chapters of this book are focused on a single driver, while others span multiple drivers. We've also included chapters that address key trends that are driving the importance of KAM, provide a comparison of KAM in the United States versus Europe, and forecast future KAM trends in life sciences.

We have designed this book to facilitate a common language and deep understanding of KAM issues and leading practices organizationwide. Some of you will read this book in its entirety, while others may focus more on select sections. The concepts shared in this book represent leading practices that are achieved in stages and over time. An understanding of these leading practices is foundational for practitioners seeking to build or transform their organization's KAM strategies, capabilities and impact. At the same time, no organization addresses all the KAM360™ drivers at once, nor moves from start-up to leading practice in a single step. It's critical to meet your organization where it is and prioritize your efforts. Which drivers you focus on and the degree of sophistication you pursue are business decisions that should be guided by an objective understanding of your current state, relative business impact, interdependencies and viability. Regardless of your stage in the journey, the insights and practices shared in this book are designed to be a valuable reference.

Throughout this book, the term key account management (KAM) should be viewed as being interchangeable with the term strategic account management (SAM). Different practitioners, academics, consultants, trainers and associations use different terms, with KAM and SAM being the most common. Since "KAM" is the more widely recognized term in the life sciences industry, we have adopted that language. In using KAM, we are purposefully referencing "key account management" and not "key account manager." KAM is an organization-wide business strategy and capability, not a role. In cases where we are discussing the key account manager role itself, we explicitly spell this out.

We also use the term "organized customer" throughout to generally refer to the healthcare provider and payer systems and groups that constitute potential key accounts for life sciences companies. Life sciences readers will note that many of the more specific customer types referenced in this book lean heavily to the U.S. market. These include integrated delivery networks (IDNs), integrated payer and provider networks (IPPNs), academic hospitals, large group practices, retail clinics, group purchasing organizations (GPOs), veterans affairs (VAs), veterans integrated services networks (VISNs), urgent care clinics, long-term care (LTC), home health agencies (HHAs), regional payers, national payers, distributors, ambulatory surgery centers and others. Although these examples are more U.S.-centric, the concepts in the book are highly relevant irrespective of region. Readers from industries other than life sciences should simply equate "organized customers" to "key accounts."

I want to extend tremendous gratitude to the many co-authors who worked so tirelessly to contribute to this book. The insights shared wouldn't be possible without their combined breadth and depth of expertise in life sciences and all things KAM. I also want to thank the many practitioners who have responded so positively to the early releases from this book and encouraged us to pursue this comprehensive publication. We've written this book for you and the many others seeking to advance their organization's KAM strategies and capabilities. Your mission has never been more important.

CHAPTER ONE

KAM is a business strategy, not a role

Mike Moorman and Namita Powers

Key account management (KAM) has become a major priority for most pharmaceutical and medtech companies for a simple reason: Organized customers such as IDNs, IPPNs, national payers, regional payers, large group practices and a host of other account types have become increasingly large, powerful and complex. Furthermore, continued horizontal and vertical integration, growing centralization of decision-making and control, less sales representative access to physicians, and more interest among organized customers in partnering with life sciences will elevate the importance of KAM even further. Life sciences companies that invest the time to get it right will protect their business and grow with these rising customers.

In this chapter, we introduce three fundamental KAM principles that stand out as particularly important considerations for life sciences leaders and that are foundational to this book:

1. KAM is a business strategy, not a role

DOI: 10.4324/9781003226512-1

2. KAM is an organization-wide initiative, not just a "sales" or "managed markets" initiative
3. KAM is a journey, not a one-time project

These core principles are central to the success of every organization that has excelled in KAM. In introducing these principles, we set the stage for the chapters to come.

PRINCIPLE NO. 1: KAM IS A BUSINESS STRATEGY, NOT A ROLE

KAM (key account management) often is mistakenly viewed as a field role (key account manager), which is a narrow view that fundamentally misses the point. KAM in life sciences is a strategy focused on providing unique offerings and value through an orchestrated, cross-functional, go-to-market model designed specifically to address the needs and engagement preferences of a defined segment of large, complex and strategically important systems and groups. KAM is dramatically different from the brand-centric and doctor-focused one-to-one engagement models that have served life sciences so well for many years and that will continue to be important in segments of the market. KAM is a many-to-many business-to-business (B2B) engagement model and requires life sciences organizations to work in new ways across their customer-facing roles and within internal functions. Creating new internal support functions and reengineering cross-functional operating models and metrics are part of the KAM equation.

To design and implement effective KAM strategies, companies should address the five core areas defined in ZS's KAM360™ framework: strategy and organization; cross-functional alignment and coordination; hiring, selection and development; metrics and motivation systems; and data and systems (Figure 1.1).

Organizations that excel in KAM approach the KAM360™ building blocks as a "recipe" and not as a "pick-and-choose menu." While

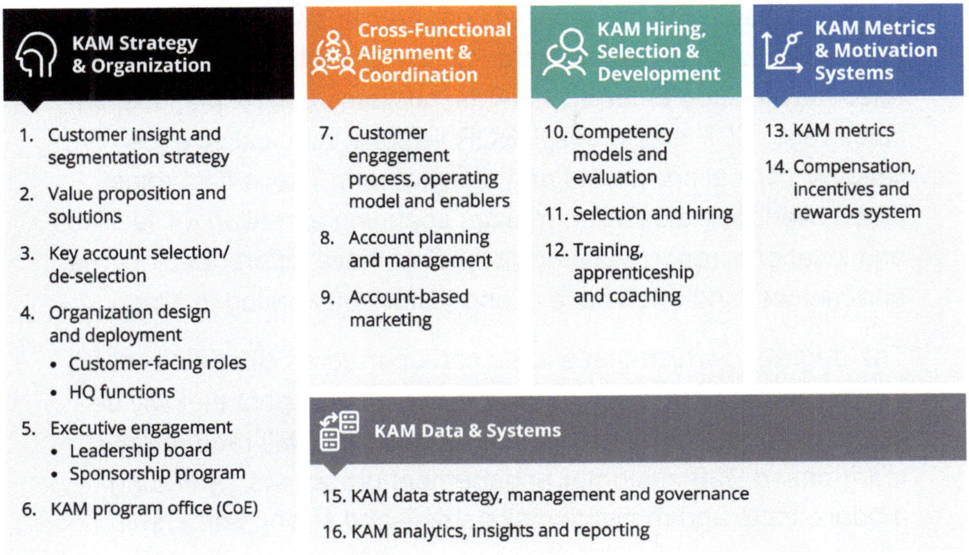

Figure 1.1 *ZS's KAM360™ framework.*

not all elements are equal priorities at any one point in time, none can be ignored.

The comprehensive KAM360™ framework underscores the notion that KAM is a business strategy—not simply a role—and is the perfect lead-in to the next principle: approaching KAM as an organization-wide capability.

PRINCIPLE NO. 2: KAM IS AN ORGANIZATION-WIDE INITIATIVE, NOT JUST A "SALES" OR "MANAGED MARKETS" INITIATIVE

KAM requires a degree of cross-functional coordination, collaboration, commitment and agility that is new to most life sciences organizations. In fact, internal silos are identified as one of the biggest barriers to KAM time and again. In other words, the real challenge is often from within.

KAM requires a diverse array of commercial and medical field roles to operate as tightly orchestrated customer-facing teams. These roles may include enterprise KAMs, business unit KAMs, hospital sales reps, HCP sales reps, HEOR liaisons, medical science liaisons, clinical specialists and many others. These field roles touch overlapping decision makers spanning a network of facilities and locations, report to different leaders, have different objectives and metrics, and often have a long history of working in silos.

The degree to which these roles can operate as close-knit teams will ultimately dictate the value and business impact that will be realized. To get there, life sciences companies will require new team-based B2B customer engagement processes, operating models, tools and motivation systems—and strong leadership alignment.

KAM also requires new and different types of internal cross-functional support spanning marketing, sales, medical, analytics, IT, human resources, training, and legal and regulatory. Many life sciences companies will need to revamp their headquarters-based functions to succeed at KAM. Take, for example, the deeply entrenched brand- and product-centric approaches that have been so successful in traditional markets and customers. KAM is about customer centricity, not brand or product centricity. Business approaches for key accounts will need to evolve from "inside out" to "outside in." KAM often requires implementing account strategy and planning, above-the-brand marketing, account-based marketing, solution support, implementation support, and specific data and tools that currently might not exist. To truly succeed at KAM, life sciences companies need to evolve their people, processes and systems organizationwide. The challenge will be "living in two worlds at once," characterized by traditional healthcare systems in some situations and rapidly evolving systems in others.

This brings us to our third core principle.

PRINCIPLE NO. 3: KAM IS A JOURNEY, NOT A ONE-TIME PROJECT

KAM has the potential to transform and improve relationships with large organized customers, but there are no shortcuts or silver bullets. Effective KAM requires many people across the organization to work in new ways, and that takes systematic effort and time. A "big bang" approach to KAM nearly always fails. The history of KAM is littered with organizations that sought to go "too big, too fast" or that thought they could excel at KAM through training and compensation alone.

Most organizations go through at least three stages on the journey to improve KAM's effectiveness, with each stage lasting about 6–18 months (Figure 1.2). In a nutshell, companies on the KAM journey begin by starting small and building a foundational capability before moving to a more advanced model and finally, building to a world-class capability.

Staging the journey doesn't preclude early wins and business impact. In fact, quite the opposite is true. By reducing complexity

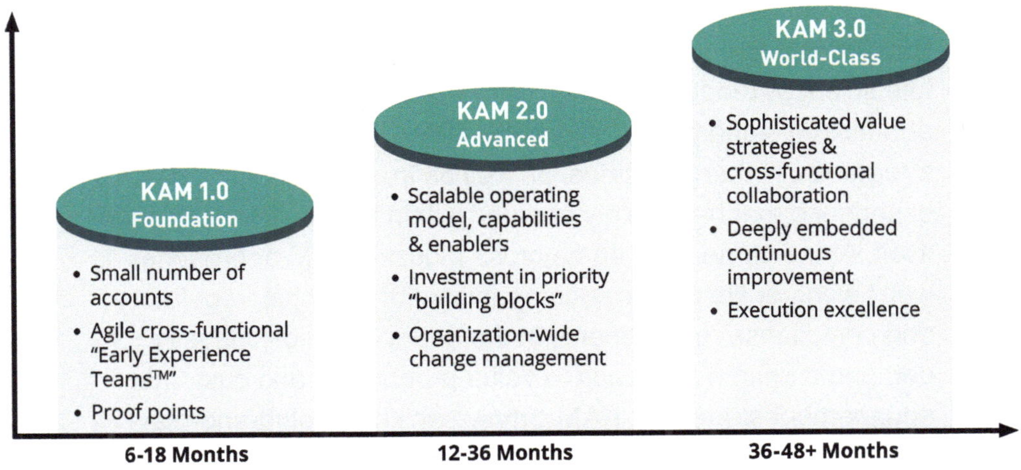

Figure 1.2 *Stages of the KAM journey.*

and focusing talent and resources, staged approaches are typically the best means to accelerate impact while simultaneously reducing risk. The successes and impact achieved at each stage of the journey create the momentum to pursue the next wave of investment and advancement.

Staging requires leaders to be highly adept at assessing where their organization is on the journey—and at defining tailored roadmaps and supporting business cases and expectations. No matter where an organization finds itself along the journey, the key is to meet the organization "where it is" and customize the path forward given the specific context and business impact opportunities.

Ultimately, KAM effectiveness and impact are all about organization-wide execution and agility. Most life sciences companies are now pursuing KAM, with many focused on advancing from KAM 1.0 to KAM 2.0, and a smaller number beginning the journey to KAM 3.0.

CONCLUDING THOUGHTS

While KAM is relatively new in the life sciences industry, many B2B industries have been pursuing KAM since the late 1980s. Life sciences leaders can learn important insights and lessons about KAM—and the KAM journey—from the successes and struggles of other industries, as well as from the substantial KAM experience that has rapidly accrued within the life sciences space itself. At the same time, some cross-industry KAM approaches won't work for life sciences companies. For example, regulatory and compliance requirements in the pharmaceutical industry demand a unique approach to value proposition and customer engagement strategies. KAM simply can't be a "plug-and-play" approach from one industry, company or business unit (BU) to the next; each iteration needs to be uniquely designed with the customer and specific company or BU in mind.

In this chapter, we have introduced three core principles for achieving KAM excellence. These principles set the stage for the remainder of this book and are worth repeating:

1. KAM is a business strategy, not a role
2. KAM is an organization-wide initiative, not just a "sales" or "managed markets" initiative
3. KAM is a journey, not a one-time project

In the chapters to come, we provide insights on how leading organizations apply these principles in practice. We explore the rise of the organized customer and KAM in life sciences, discuss in detail the components of the KAM360™ framework and review the current and future state of KAM in the industry. Our intention is to provide insights that can be leveraged at any stage of the journey, whether that is building a new KAM program or advancing an existing program to world-class status.

CHAPTER TWO

The rise of the organized customer and KAM in healthcare

Brian Chapman and Pratap Khedkar

For life sciences companies, the clinician—predominantly the physician writing a drug script or the surgeon doing a procedure—was traditionally the most significant decision-maker within the healthcare ecosystem. Given the freedom that clinicians had to make individual choices on behalf of patients as they saw fit, they were consequently the center of pharma and medtech company sales and marketing efforts. In a clinician-centric world, healthcare institutions operated largely in the background, relatively insensitive to price and inclined to treat life sciences as innovation suppliers.

But this model has shifted dramatically. No longer are individual doctors the primary decision-makers when it comes to many life sciences products. Institutions—or large "organized customers"—have assumed a far greater role in actively managing these purchasing decisions to drive greater clinical, financial,

DOI: 10.4324/9781003226512-2

patient-experience and healthcare provider work-life outcomes. And this shift has had significant implications for how life sciences companies broadly promote and sell their offerings, as well as for the role key account management (KAM) plays in engaging these entities more specifically.

In this chapter, we discuss the emergence and rise of the organized customer and how life sciences companies can overcome these customers' heterogeneity to successfully implement KAM strategies and provide value.

WHAT IS AN ORGANIZED CUSTOMER?

To understand the rise of organized customers, it's helpful to first look at the healthcare ecosystem, which includes an array of players interacting across the value chain to provide healthcare to the patient. In this ecosystem, funding, management, service delivery and product manufacturing are split across entire industry sub-verticals (Figure 2.1).

Each of these groups includes a bewildering variety of players with different focus areas and characteristics. For example, funding comes not only from large government agencies, but also from employers and patients themselves via their co-pays. Health plans moreover may bear risk or simply concentrate on utilization management on behalf of employers. And providers can work independently or as parts of highly complicated integrated delivery networks.

For our purposes, organized customers are any institutional entities in the healthcare ecosystem that make consolidated decisions beyond those of an individual clinician or their practice. This definition includes government agencies such as the U.S. Centers for Medicare & Medicaid Services (CMS), state Medicaid

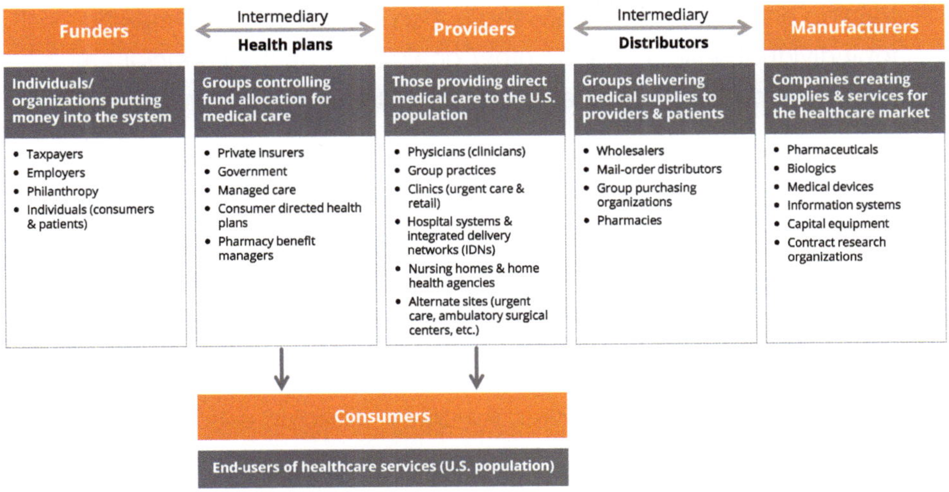

Figure 2.1 *The U.S. healthcare system at a glance.*

or, in other countries, entities such as the National Health Service in England. It also comprises insurance companies such as UnitedHealthcare; regional payers like Blue Cross Blue Shield of Florida; pharmacy benefit managers such as Optum (a subsidiary of UnitedHealth Group); hospital systems like the Cleveland Clinic or HCA Healthcare; and very large practice networks such as Florida Cancer Specialists & Research Institute. Determining which of these organized customer types to engage through KAM is a strategic decision and will vary from one company or region to another.

Attempts to characterize the players in simple terms (such as payers, health plans, providers, delivery networks and affiliates) can be seductive but also misleading. Vertical consolidation across these entities has blurred the lines between many of these players. Organized customers can be multi-faceted conglomerates, rivaling or even dominating the size of the largest pharmaceutical and medtech companies that serve them. Hospital systems can be the largest employer in their cities and exert major regional influence in state capitals. What ultimately characterizes the organized customer is the presence of a professional class of managers whose training or incentives are focused not on clinical decision-making for individual patients but on other goals such as the financial performance or operational efficiency of the whole organization.

Institutional players in the healthcare ecosystem have always been "organized" in the strict sense of the word—and, in fact, many have existed for decades. But previously, these customers weren't particularly interested in engaging with life sciences companies, nor did they feel a compelling reason to tell clinicians what they could and couldn't do.

Today's landscape is different. A variety of factors—especially including the opportunity to improve clinical, financial and experience outcomes—have led these organizations to show a new side to pharma and medtech companies, which now need to think more broadly about "customers" in the healthcare ecosystem. In the United States, for instance, the past 10 years have seen a dramatic change in organized customers' priorities and a subsequent waning of clinicians' individual decision-making abilities. Clinical stakeholders who once were the sole decision-maker now have organizations looking over their shoulders, influencing those decisions for either clinical, economic or experience reasons that need to be balanced along with clinicians' own judgment. The rise of the organized customer and the associated shift in needs, objectives and operating models has changed the game for life sciences companies. KAM is now a critical organization-wide business strategy and capability for engaging complex institutions, not just individual clinicians.

THE ORIGIN OF THE RISE

The emergence of organized customers hasn't been abrupt. We can trace the rise of the organized customer in the U.S. healthcare system, for example, to several important environmental and market events over more than a decade that have driven—and accelerated—the trend.

GOVERNMENT

The arrival of Medicare Part D in 2006 was an important first inflection point, especially for the pharmaceutical industry. By covering the drug costs for millions of Americans, Part D motivated health plan administrators to identify new ways to manage costs and drug utilization to maximize profit. Influencing and standardizing individual clinical decisions became an administrative priority—one that rippled through the healthcare system—particularly in primary care. The Affordable Care Act of 2010 (the ACA) and legislation such as the Medicare Access and CHIP Reauthorization Act (MACRA) further shifted the way providers were reimbursed—moving from a "fee for service" model where providers are paid for each visit, drug, or procedure to "value-based payments" where financial incentives are used to encourage quality care, usually defined as improved outcomes or lower costs.[1] These value-based payment schemes were pioneered by Medicare through vehicles such as accountable care organizations (ACOs) and were quickly copied by private-sector insurers. As providers strategized ways to profit under these new payment schemes, they quickly realized that the best way to achieve "quality" was through increased volume and standardization of care delivery[2]—the latter requiring infrastructure investments such as system-wide unified electronic health records (EHR). Scale became an advantage for providers and drove many years of health systems mergers and acquisition of clinics in surrounding geographies. The result was many of the large, controlling organized providers we observe today.

HOSPITAL MARGINS

A second trend that has accelerated the rise of organized customers is the pressure on hospitals themselves, which since 2015 have become increasingly unprofitable. Before the COVID-19 pandemic, hospitals' median profit margin was 3.5%, meaning healthcare delivery was becoming less viable—especially as a for-profit enterprise. As diagnosis-related groups are reviewed and adjusted and as the inpatient procedure exclusion list shrinks and more procedures move to settings of lower acuity, hospitals have had to look for more opportunities to cut costs or to boost revenue. Pharma and medtech companies are expected to respond.

HIGH-COST INNOVATION

Healthcare is also becoming increasingly expensive. Unlike in many areas of consumer technology (for example, computers, personal tech devices and televisions) where innovation often leads to lower costs and better accessibility, healthcare has moved in the opposite direction with respect to innovation. Rather than reducing costs, the vast majority of healthcare innovation is designed to prolong life, to extend treatments to underserved conditions and, especially, to treat rare conditions. This focus has certainly resulted in better patient outcomes, but at a higher cost of care. In fact, the growing cost of healthcare innovation is, in part, responsible for the cost of care far outstripping GDP in the western world year after year. At the same time, the healthcare system's collective budget hasn't expanded commensurately, driving healthcare administrators to become better organized when interacting with life sciences companies. Together these trends have highlighted a fundamental misalignment between user, payer and decision-maker that often exists.

HORIZONTAL CONSOLIDATION IN INSURERS

Consolidation among U.S. insurers, in part as a response to the aforementioned pressures, has further contributed to the rise in organized customers. There are now essentially five insurers in the United States, each pursuing its own strategies and consolidation. This consolidation can be even more dramatic at the local level, where typically a subset of those five entities is actually viable within any given market—meaning that only one to three payers are present in some local healthcare ecosystems. This high degree of consolidation inevitably leads to even more organization in local-level decision-making.

CONSOLIDATION AMONG HOSPITALS

Hospital mergers have also been an important factor, perhaps in response to the ACA or at least accelerated by it. These combinations aren't limited to single hospitals, but extend to IDNs, either through formal ownership or mechanisms like alliances, collaborations and management agreements. IDNs have continued to consolidate with no end in sight.

VERTICAL INTEGRATION

Further complexity has emerged with vertical integration across the players in the healthcare space. In recent years, we've seen payers branch into providers, PBMs, specialty pharmacy and even care delivery in surgery centers—basically everywhere except the hospital itself. Hospitals, through IDNs, have merged vertically across sites of care by buying practices and investing in home care, rehab and ambulatory surgery, creating an even stronger network to rival the power of the payers and patients they serve. In some ways, vertical consolidation has led to exponentially more complexity because of the number of organizational-structure permutations it creates. In fact, complexity is the name of the game within U.S. healthcare now and a big reason why life sciences companies need to engage through KAM.

MAKING SENSE OF ORGANIZED CUSTOMERS' HETEROGENEITY

The complexity and diversity of organized customers leave pharma and medtech companies without a simple taxonomy to define the companies they're targeting. Organized customers in general, especially large ones, look very different from one another in their degree of vertical integration, relative power in local markets and overarching goals—and should therefore be engaged with a bespoke approach. How can pharma and medtech companies overcome this heterogeneity to successfully implement their KAM strategy? The **Structure, Intent, Expression (SIE) framework** can help pharma and medtech companies apply three distinct lenses to address this heterogeneity productively and adapt their engagement strategies accordingly.

"Structure" characterizes an organized customer's scope and organization design. Structure reflects an organized customer's strategic focus (the segment of the healthcare value chain it concentrates on and how it intends to extract value) and includes the systems, infrastructure and operating-model investments made to execute on that strategy (such as operational scale, integration of operations across facilities and sites of care, and physician and IT infrastructure). By examining an organized customer's structure, pharma and medtech companies can gain insight into the customer's priorities. For example, an organized customer that owns a health plan, a pharmacy and a surgical care center—all of which are driven by a single, integrated EHR system—can coordinate care across these sites, which is a prerequisite for having any kind of intent or expression of control.

"Intent" characterizes an organized customer's therapeutic area and service line-level objectives. An institution often pays lip service to the many elements of outcomes, patient experience, staff experience and financial results but, in reality, usually focuses only on a subset of these issues within a narrow range of therapy areas or service lines at any given time. For example, research and education may be the focus of one IDN that considers reputational prestige and solutions for rare-disease patients more important than pure cost savings. Another organization might prioritize throughput and providing highly accessible affordable care over caring for the most difficult and rare patients. A third organization, one that also has an associated payer component, may be more focused on the holistic patient and on providing care not just in the hospital but across the entire site of care given its responsibility as payers. These high-level objectives will have downstream impacts on many of the purchasing decisions related to pharma and medtech products. For example, a health system's focus on a particular therapy area will impact which of the many drug classes it uses and for which it centrally influences usage. Similarly, which specific features of a medical device a health system values most, or whether the system centralizes its purchases from one manufacturer or spreads them among many, can be a function of how that system's administration balances lowering cost with accessing the latest clinical innovations. By understanding an organized customers' intent, pharma and medtech companies can more effectively align with those objectives.

"Expression" measures the extent to which an organized customer actually achieves its intent. For instance, an organization that employs its doctors, measures their utilization and standardizes care across locations might be measurably successful in its efforts to reduce costs, improve outcomes or increase patient satisfaction. Other organized customers may have the same stated intent, but in practice may not have implemented the mechanisms necessary to succeed (for example, they continue to let clinicians act autonomously). Expression—the demonstrated ability to achieve intent—is the final piece of the puzzle that determines whether an organized customer can impact the use of a life sciences company's product or solution.

There are two practically useful reasons to view organized customers through the lens of structure, intent and expression. The first is that these three factors represent a natural progression. An organized customer generally makes a change or investment in "structure" to gain new capabilities (for example, UnitedHealth

Group acquires Optum or a health system invests in a unified EHR system across all its sites of care). The customer would then select an "intent"—a category on which to focus these capabilities—and either succeed or not in driving a change in the care paradigm as "expressed" by measurable results. The progressive nature of these capabilities gives pharma and medtech companies an opportunity to anticipate future changes. The second reason this framework is useful is that "expression" is very hard to measure on its own. Even with robust data on the behavioral patterns within an institution, it's difficult to know if those patterns are due to central control. Of the approximately 6,000 hospitals in the United States, some will appear to behave differently than others purely due to randomness. However, adding both structure and intent boosts confidence that any expression observed is real and not just an aberration of data. The SIE framework is a solution to a very complex problem: how to characterize the many heterogeneous and interdependent organized customers operating in the complex healthcare ecosystem.

CONCLUDING THOUGHTS

The rise of the organized customer coincides with the imperative to improve outcomes in a combination of essential areas: clinical, financial, patient experience and healthcare provider work life. Historically, most organized customers have allowed clinicians to operate independently and have regarded life sciences companies as not much more than suppliers. But as needs and priorities have shifted, business and operating models have evolved. Organized customers are centralizing decision-making and increasing control over individual clinician choice—and they are expecting pharma and medtech companies to find new ways to help them achieve their objectives.

To succeed, life sciences companies must embrace business-to-business KAM as a primary go-to-market strategy while continuing to promote to clinicians. They'll need both models to coexist and synergistically reinforce one another. In pursuing KAM, life sciences must find ways to create value in the ecosystem as they engage with the organized customer. While the definition of "value" in life sciences can be a charged discussion that invokes regulatory and compliance considerations, the notion of providing value through superior customer experience and advanced solutions is a critical aspect of KAM. The definition of value will change based on the context, the customer type and what can legally be done within the confines of compliance. Still, there's plenty of room for life sciences companies to bring forward both new ways of engaging organized customers and advanced solutions that address critical needs within the healthcare ecosystem. Life sciences companies that excel at KAM will use KAM as a competitive advantage and eventually become market leaders.

NOTES

1 Tingyin T. Chee et al., "Current State of Value-Based Purchasing Programs," Circulation 133, no. 22 (May 31, 2016): 2197–2205, https://doi.org/10.1161/CIRCULATIONAHA.115.010268.
2 American Hospital Association, "Hospital Mergers: Foundation for a Modern, Efficient and High-Performing Health Care System of the Future," December 2018, https://www.aha.org/system/files/2018-12/executive-summary-hospital-merger-benefits-a-review-and-extension_0.pdf.

CHAPTER THREE

Where to play: Key account segmentation and selection

Joe Stevens and Jude Konzelmann

In life sciences, the concept of organized customer segmentation goes in and out of fashion every few years. At times, it seems like the term "segmentation" itself is overused, then is replaced by slight changes in methodology and often an interim period of new terminology (such as "archetype" or "cluster"). Despite the fickleness of popular opinion, however, understanding the customer remains one of the fundamentals of developing and executing an effective key account management (KAM) strategy. Before a company can design a strategy for mutual value creation, it must know what a customer needs—i.e., the landscape upon which any value for that customer gets created. Also, it's important to understand the customer's willingness and ability to work with the company, and if the customer is sufficiently important to engage with KAM. This is all about figuring out "where to play," which is a prerequisite to identifying "how to win." This chapter

DOI: 10.4324/9781003226512-3

is devoted to developing a systematic understanding of the customer segments and accounts that warrant a KAM strategy and approach.

THE THREE LEVELS OF ORGANIZED CUSTOMER SEGMENTATION

The modern life sciences manufacturer engages with many different organized customers. In the United States, this almost always includes payers and provider organizations. But often, it also includes group purchasing organizations (GPOs), pharmacy benefit managers (PBMs), large dialysis organizations (LDOs) and many other networks, depending on the therapy areas or service lines in which a particular company competes. The U.S. healthcare industry has also developed a long and sometimes confusing list of acronyms for organized customers—for example, an "accountable care organization," which is only an organization in the loosest sense of the term. A partial list of these entities and associated acronyms for some of the most important organized customer types is noted in Table 3.1.

While many of these types of organizations are likely to warrant a KAM approach, each play a very different role in the healthcare system—and the optimal KAM model differs across these organizations in important ways. For example, key account managers engaged at a payer or PBM might manage the process of negotiating rebates in exchange for formulary status, while a key account manager at an IDN might deliver an improved education program for the IDN's staff or a revision of the IDN's discharge protocol for a patient type.

Most life sciences companies will first segment their account universe by "type of account" and then split their organization structures accordingly in acknowledgment of the different

Table 3.1 *Important organized customer types in the U.S. healthcare system*

Integrated delivery network (IDN)	A health system that integrates at least one primary and one acute care facility with the goal of logically integrating healthcare delivery. An IDN may also integrate various specialty care facilities or a health insurer under the same corporate structure. Some IDNs operate nationally, but many focus in one or more specific regions.
Integrated payer provider network (IPPN)	An IDN that also owns its own health insurer.
Accountable care organization (ACO)	A Medicare payment mechanism by which one or more healthcare providers agree to accept value-based payments for the services they provide. An ACO isn't an actual "organization" in the traditional sense (ACOs do not directly employ doctors, but practices can be members). This structure is often copied by states and private-sector insurers (for instance, "commercial ACOs"), sometimes using different names.
Managed care organization (MCO)	A collection of healthcare providers that have agreed to provide care under a specific set of financial terms. MCOs are more commonly referred to as a "health plan."
Management services organization (MSO)	An outsourced administrative service provided to physician practices that often handles issues surrounding reimbursement, billing, payments and similar functions.
Pharmacy benefit manager (PBM)	An organization that manages the pharmacy benefit portion of a health plan (such as drugs dispensed at retail pharmacies).
Group purchasing organization (GPO)	An entity that negotiates with manufacturers on behalf of a large number of smaller healthcare providers to obtain favorable rates through purchasing at a larger volume.
Large dialysis organization (LDO)	A very large healthcare provider dedicated to providing dialysis services to patients with end-stage renal disease.
Ambulatory surgical center (ASC)	A dedicated site where outpatient surgery is performed. ASCs may be affiliated with a larger system such as an IDN.

(*Continued*)

The U.S. Department of Veterans Affairs (VA)	In healthcare, this refers to the government-sponsored insurance services and dedicated provider organizations that serve members of the armed forces and their families.
Home health agencies (HHA)	A person or group certified by the U.S. Centers for Medicare & Medicaid Services (CMS) to provide healthcare services outside of a hospital or clinic.
Long-term care (LTC) and skilled nursing facilities (SNF)	An in-patient care provider that focuses on patients who need healthcare services over a long period of time, such as the elderly, the disabled or patients in rehabilitation.
Risk-bearing medical groups	Medical groups that participate in value-based payment systems such as ACOs or the oncology care model (OCM).

strategies, objectives, activities and accompanying skills required of account managers in each function. Broadly, this split is often accomplished through the creation of three buckets: "payer-like" accounts (including MCOs, PBMs and IPPNs), "provider-like" accounts (including IDNs, LDOs and risk-bearing medical groups) and "government accounts" (including Medicare, Medicaid and the VA or the Department of Defense).

Not all accounts will fit cleanly into this categorization. It's not uncommon to have a team covering more than one account type in small organizations (for instance, a single team calling on both payers and providers) or multiple teams focused on a single account type in large organizations (for instance, separate teams for IDNs and alternative sites of care). But logically, the biggest differences in engagement objectives and customer-facing activities occur among these three groups. We often refer to this as a "Level 1" segmentation (Figure 3.1).

The second level of account segmentation usually occurs within each of these larger groups based on account characteristics such as potential, needs, control and partnership orientation. Here, differences among customers are less obvious at first glance. For

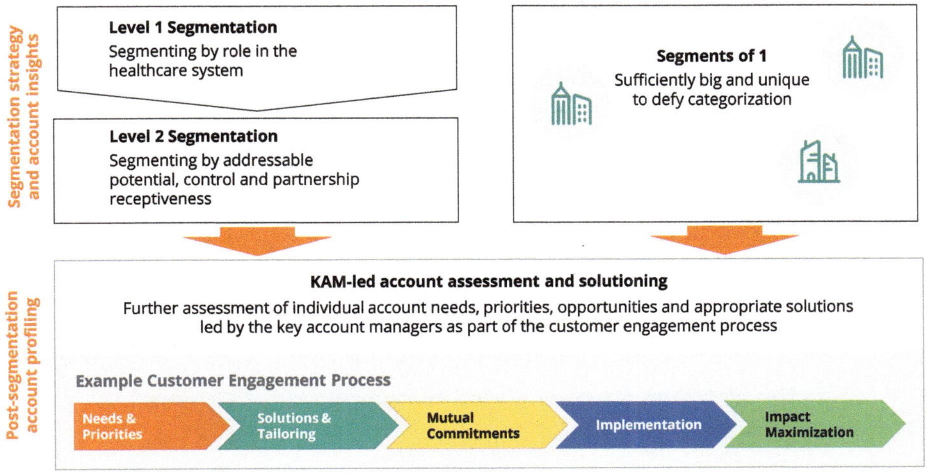

Figure 3.1 *Customer segmentation levels.*

example, it's easy to see that a payer like UnitedHealth Group might need different engagement than a health system like Sharp Healthcare, but less easy to understand how Sharp Healthcare's needs might differ from Intermountain Healthcare's without more deeply understanding each of the two providers. Variables such as overall market potential, the degree of control and centralized decision-making, and their willingness to partner with life sciences manufacturers all significantly affect how a manufacturer should engage with a customer.

For this reason, Level 2 segmentation usually leverages one or more secondary data sources. For example, a company might collect profile data such as number of beds and sophistication of electronic health record (EHR) systems and combine it with information on claims processed in the customer's therapy areas or service lines to help separate these similar accounts into relevant groups. Sorting accounts into these groups is done generally for two reasons. The first is "account selection," or separating the account universe into accounts the company will target with key account teams and those it won't. The second is to create a tiering and prioritization of the accounts to target.

Here's an example of one common key account tiering approach:

- **Tier 1: Strategic accounts.** These are the closest, most consistently engaged customers that are critical to the company's business and active in managing the company's category. Strategic accounts are often the partners with which the company develops innovative ideas or co-creates bespoke solutions to challenging problems, although smaller, more nimble key accounts can sometimes be good candidates for this as well. A company generally has the smallest number of accounts in the strategic account segment compared with others.
- **Tier 2: Key accounts.** Often just as important to the company's business as strategic accounts, key accounts are distinguished by being slightly less focused on the company's category or not as inclined to partner with life sciences manufacturers. These accounts still receive plenty of attention from key account managers but would less often co-create a bespoke solution and more often tailor solutions from a predefined menu. Key accounts usually outnumber strategic accounts, as even a large company can only engage with a small number of accounts as true strategic partners.
- **Tier 3: Monitored accounts.** Customers in this tier may share some similarities with strategic or key accounts but are usually missing at least one quality that would place them in the higher tiers. For example, perhaps the account doesn't focus on the company's category as a target for control or centralized decision-making, or it may not have a strong partnership orientation or capability with the company in the past. In general, monitored accounts still receive a KAM approach, but in a more reactive way with less effort. This tier generally has the largest number of accounts, each with the potential to one day become a key or strategic account.

As illustrated in the upper-right of Figure 3.1, it's important to note that some customers—such as Kaiser Permanente, UnitedHealth

Group and the VA—are outliers when it comes to segmentation and warrant a "segment of 1" approach. These accounts are so large that they're systemically important to a company's business and so unique that a special value strategy, engagement model, set of skills and knowledge are needed to succeed with them. While these customers are complex and hard to understand, their high value to the business means they are usually worth separating from the rest for individual attention—i.e., a "segment of 1"—and getting specifically devoted resources for insight collection, strategy development and engagement.

Irrespective of segmentation approach and associated account insights, the key account team will always need to further assess individual account needs, priorities, opportunities and solutions as part of the customer engagement process. The quip "If you've seen one hospital, you've seen one hospital" is an industry cliché but remains true—and the sentiment applies to almost any type of large organized customer. A well-executed segmentation approach will take a company most of the way toward understanding customer needs and defining its segment-specific value strategies and engagement models. But intimate customer insight is achieved through expert execution of the customer engagement process by individual key account managers and account team members. While accounts in the same Level 2 segment should share a generally similar set of needs, some accounts will always prioritize their needs differently. Accounts can also be at different levels of maturity, which can make a specific offering more or less attractive to that account at a particular time. Consider, for example, two similar IDNs both trying to standardize care delivery across their physicians. One might highly value education programs, while the other might look to implement its desired care pathways in its EHR. The need is the same, but how each IDN fulfills that need is a function of its history, institutional culture and other competing priorities at any given time. The key account manager is best placed to understand, adapt to and influence these factors.

USING DATA TO SYSTEMATICALLY ASSESS LEVEL 2 CHARACTERISTICS

In the framework described in Figure 3.1, ease of segmentation across the two levels isn't uniform. Level 1 segments are easily observable, often by just looking at the name of the institution. Level 2 segmentation—which is focused on account characteristics such as potential, needs, control and partnership orientation—is generally where it's the most difficult to develop good insights. A major challenge with Level 2 segmentation is the high degree of variability in these characteristics across a large number of accounts and the difficulty of establishing accurate measures of each. Data is critical to generating these insights.

In general, three dimensions most strongly influence account prioritization within a Level 2 segmentation: addressable potential, control and partnership receptiveness (Figure 3.2). "Addressable

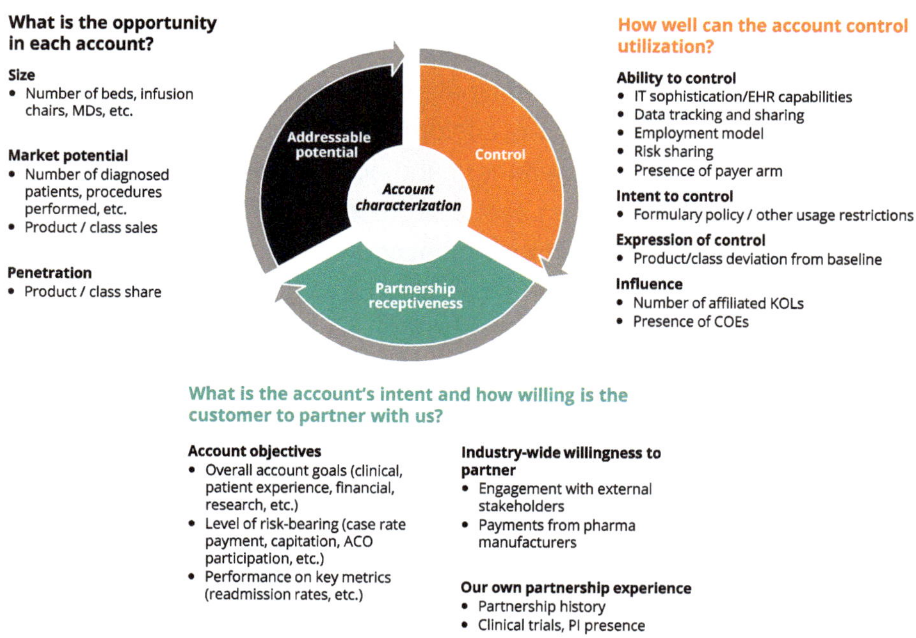

Figure 3.2 *Dimensions of a Level 2 segmentation.*

potential" is intended to quantify the future sales volume the company could achieve at that account. In most cases, this can be easily measured by looking at the total patient volume or procedures from affiliated physicians (such as total sales of a market basket of products or total diagnosed patients), although sometimes other metrics such as number of physicians of a specialty or the company's market share can also be incorporated. In general, most companies have a well-defined metric for addressable potential, which can be used for Level 2 segmentation as well. A common mistake companies make, however, is to only look at this single metric when selecting and tiering their target accounts. A large account that doesn't centrally organize to exert control over its affiliated physicians or individual hospitals—or that isn't inclined to work together with the company—shouldn't be a top-tier customer because there won't be sufficient opportunity to create mutual value. It's these factors the next two dimensions are designed to address.

The "control" dimension reflects business needs and priorities and is intended to capture the extent to which centralized administrative decisions affect the use of the company's products. Even if an account has a large volume passing through it, that account is only an important customer for KAM if it has centralized decision-making in a way that influences how the company's products are purchased and used. However, due to differences in the nature of control across therapy areas and service lines, the meaning of "high control" and "low control" must be assessed at the therapy-area and service-line level.

For example, in the past, health system administrators had very little influence on the use of retail drugs (that is, drugs for which a patient received a prescription and picked up at the drug store). Retail prescribing was historically just a function of the physician to write the prescription and the patient's payer to approve or deny the claim at the pharmacy. We've started to see some examples of influence on retail prescribing, but it's usually limited to a handful of high-cost therapy areas at the most sophisticated institutions—ones that often bear financial risk for the patient and have advanced EHR systems to help them enforce these policies. We would define these sophisticated systems as "high control," while systems that don't exert influence on the prescribing physician would qualify as "low control." In contrast, purchases of large radiological or surgical equipment is a significant capital expenditure and almost always driven by administration rather than individual physicians. In these cases, we might define high-control accounts as those making centralized decisions for multiple hospitals, while low-control accounts don't coordinate across the system and instead allow individual hospitals to make their own choices. In both cases, the implication for a KAM program is the same: An account's value is more than just the number of patients, procedures or prescriptions associated with that institution. The most important accounts for a KAM program are those that are not only large but centrally control the use of the company's products.

Similar to the SIE (Structure, Intent and Expression) framework discussed in the previous chapter for understanding the heterogeneity of organized customers, we generally think about control in three ways:

- **Ability to control** encompasses the presence of the administrative and technological infrastructure required to influence physician behavior (this is usually the same for a given institution regardless of therapy area or service line). Ability to control is often a function of observable traits, such as whether a health system uses a single EHR or employs its physicians.
- **Intent to control** reflects category-level objectives for specific therapy areas and service lines (i.e., what they are trying to achieve at the category level and how). This can be assessed by examining which management tools are applied to a specific therapy area or service line.

- **Expression of control** measures the degree to which those objectives are being achieved. Estimation of expression often focuses on the deviation in usage of a given life sciences company's specific product or class of products against a baseline of expected usage.

By evaluating ability, intent and expression in this way, a life sciences company can accurately describe the differences between institutions and effectively identify the high- and low-control accounts in any product category.

The third dimension, "partnership receptiveness," measures an organized customer's desire and ability to meaningfully engage with life sciences manufacturers. A key consideration is the account's objectives and if the company's offerings can help the account to achieve them. Also important is the account's willingness to work together. Some organized customers have a higher receptivity to partnership purely as a function of their leadership, organizational culture or strategy. For example, if a medical device manufacturer is looking to help its customers with practice-building activities such as offering a new procedure or attracting new patients, this dimension should capture the provider traits that would make a customer receptive to these offerings. Sometimes, intangible factors such as institutional strategy or culture also play a role. The insurer Harvard Pilgrim Health Care, for instance, has long been viewed as excited to engage in value-based contracts with pharmaceutical companies, despite being demographically similar to many other small regional payers. Whenever possible, this dimension should also capture elements that are unique to the company. Identifying where the company has engaged successfully in the past, where it has particularly strong individual relationships with senior leadership or where it has broader organizational relationships through non-commercial activities such as clinical trials can help a company pinpoint where it can more successfully engage through KAM.

PUTTING IT ALL TOGETHER

What do these principles look like in practice? In this section, we examine two real-life examples in which ZS was involved and discuss the specific insights a Level 2 segmentation can generate.

EXAMPLE 1: A RELATIVELY SIMPLE SEGMENTATION OF NATIONAL AND REGIONAL U.S. MANAGED CARE ORGANIZATIONS FOR A PAYER KAM FUNCTION

The first example involves a company that was launching a moderately differentiated new product into a well-established therapy area populated by a variety of branded and generic products. The goal of the company's key account engagement was to gain formulary access with payers to eliminate any barriers to the sales force's efforts to promote the new product to physicians and to encourage prescription of the product to patients who would benefit. Existing products in this market were heavily contracted and contract negotiation was the primary lever the KAM team could leverage to gain access. The straightforward nature of customer needs ("good financial terms") and key account manager activities ("contract negotiation") called for a relatively simple approach (Figure 3.3).

A database of covered lives by payer and anonymized patient claims data linked to each payer provided the information needed to create an index that ranked payers by their market potential, which formed the first segmentation dimension. For the second dimension, we looked at each payer's formulary policies to identify the level of restrictiveness (the payer's "intent" to influence prescribing) and then the degree to which that payer's patients were prescribed drugs that followed the policies (how effectively the payer "expressed" control). The combination of these two

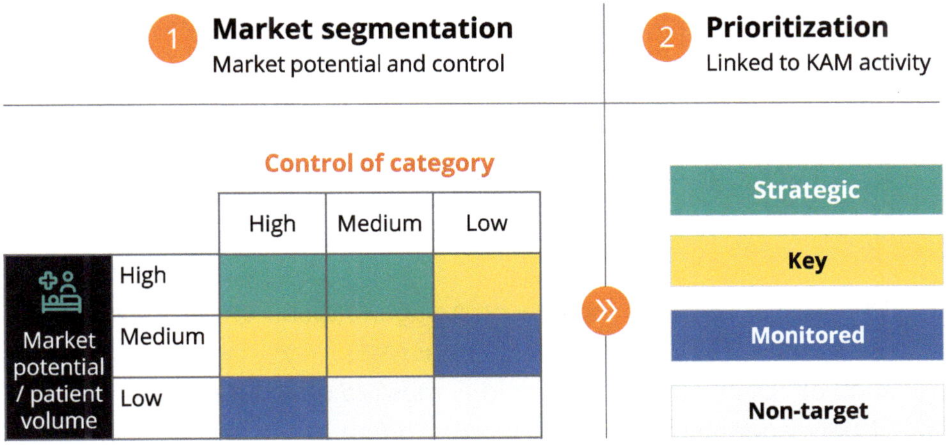

Figure 3.3 *Simple segmentation of national and regional payers across two dimensions.*

dimensions provided an actionable framework for the account team to engage with these payers at launch.

A relatively small number of very large payers and PBMs, which also tended to exert high or medium levels of control, occupied the "high" value segment. These accounts are so large that the company's product couldn't have succeeded without at least some formulary access. These must-win accounts became the "strategic account" tier and the highest-priority focus, receiving the most leadership attention and senior key account managers.

The accounts that were either large with low control or medium in size with moderate to high control made up the second ("key account") tier. While less of a focus than the "strategic account" tier, these accounts were assigned a key account manager tasked with maintaining a steady relationship and proactively attempting to negotiate a contract granting favorable access. Finally, moderately sized accounts with low control and small accounts with high control were assigned key account managers who introduced themselves at launch and shared some product information but made no proactive attempt to secure a contract (that is, a contract would only be discussed if the account asked for it directly).

EXAMPLE 2: A SEGMENTATION OF PROVIDER ORGANIZATIONS INVOLVING ADDITIONAL COMPLEXITY

The second example focuses on a segmentation of organized providers. The account universe contained mostly health systems, such as IDNs, but this terminology masked a high degree of heterogeneity in these customers' organization structure, sophistication and needs. Additionally, the company was a large pharma manufacturer with a diverse portfolio that included products ranging from mass-market to rare diseases, and a mix of orals, injectables and infusions. This led to additional complexity in both the segmentation itself and how it would be used.

The first dimension, market potential, was conceptually the same as in the simpler payer example, except that more therapy areas were included in the index. For the "control of category" dimension, however, the analysis became more complex. In the previous payer example, the company leveraged a database of formulary policies for each payer as a straightforward measure of the level of control. For provider organizations, no such consolidated database is currently available, so instead the company looked for the presence of institutional sophistication that indicated control would be possible—for example, an integrated EHR system, direct employment of physicians and risk-bearing activity such as participation in an ACO or selling an insurance plan on the exchanges. By the same token, since the data on institutional policy doesn't exist, the company evaluated expression of control by comparing prescribing patterns to a national and regional baseline, as well as by looking for "homogeneity" within the physicians affiliated with an institution (for instance, whether those physicians all prescribed pharmaceuticals in the same way across sites of care within a system or behaved differently from one another).

The "partnership receptiveness" dimension also became much more important in this second example. This dimension was largely ignored in the prior payer example because "willingness to receive a rebate" is mostly universal among payers and being a "high control" payer usually signified an account that was already actively contracting with one of the company's competitors. In this second example, the company had a large number of existing relationships with the accounts being examined, which included clinical development, medical and commercial stakeholders. Additionally, a wide range of programs were already in place with many of these providers, including education programs, real-world evidence gathering, investigator-initiated trials and value-based contracts. A wealth of data was available on historical engagements, from which the company could predict the likelihood that an account would be willing to work closely with the company in the future. This information was supplemented with proxy metrics measuring the degree to which each account had invested in initiatives around patient experience, clinical-outcome improvement and cost savings. These combined metrics used to estimate partnership receptiveness became an important third axis of the segmentation.

The results of this segmentation (Figure 3.4), similar to the first example, influenced which accounts the key account team would engage with and how much they focused on each account. But the segmentation also heavily influenced the value strategy and engagement process for each account. The top segment, strategic accounts, was offered the most comprehensive set of advanced solutions and was seen as a fertile ground for the co-creation of new ideas. This group was targeted for complex and higher investment programs such as real-world evidence generation and development of innovative contracting approaches. The next segment, key accounts, received very similar treatment as the strategic accounts,

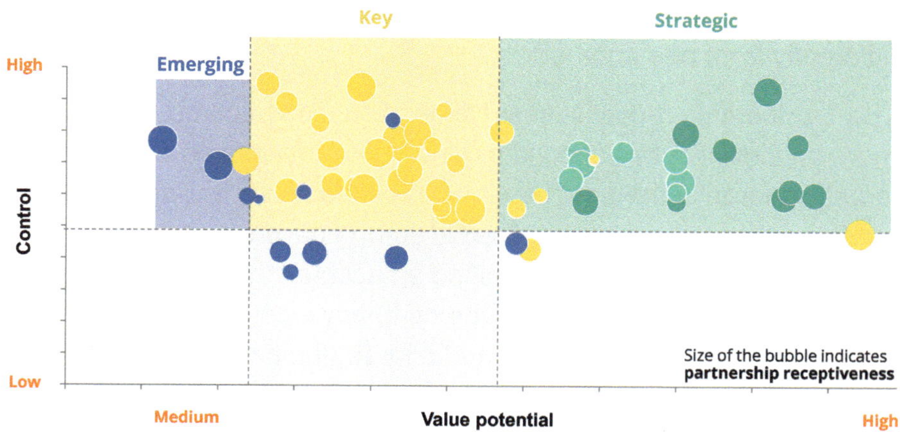

Figure 3.4 *Complex provider organization segmentation example.*

except they tended to be brought solution ideas that had been developed as a menu by segment marketing as opposed to being offered opportunities to shape the idea from the beginning. Finally, a third segment of emerging accounts was engaged with a subset of the offerings made available to the higher tiers—mainly focused on education and bringing institutions up to modern standards of care. Note that non-target accounts were excluded prior to the analysis.

In considering these examples, it's important to remember that while the general concepts of addressable potential, control and partnership receptiveness will apply in almost all cases, the definition of each of these concepts and the resulting segments will differ significantly by type of account being segmented, category of product being sold and therapy area or service line in which those products are used. Our examples show how measures of control differ according to available data from payers and providers. It's common for measures of addressable potential to differ significantly by category—for example, in an established pharmaceutical market, a company tends to look at a basket of competitor products; in the case of a medical device, it might look at total number of procedures; and in orphan diseases, there may be no existing products and diagnosis might be inconsistent, so proxies such as the number of beds or covered lives might be used. The output from a segmentation is often even more different. For example, the very large hospital systems such as HCA Healthcare might be the most important key account for the manufacturer of an implantable device but may not be a KAM target for an organization focused on a retail pharmaceutical. While we have shared some general examples here, they're far from comprehensive. The definition of each dimension in such a segmentation must be tailored to each individual situation and use case.

HANDLING THE "SEGMENTS OF 1"

Our discussion to this point has focused on taking a universe of tens or hundreds of accounts and separating them into groups with similar characteristics and needs within groups while differing across groups. But some institutions, because of their size and uniqueness, defy this type of categorization. As indicated earlier, we call these "segments of 1" to indicate that it doesn't really make sense to group them with anyone else. Let's look at some examples of the defining characteristics that make these accounts so unique and difficult to classify and, thus, create the need to handle them differently.

The first type of account to consider here is one like Kaiser Permanente, a well-known system with roots in Northern California that now has outposts across the country. What makes Kaiser so unique is its degree of vertical integration and how strictly it's isolated from the rest of the healthcare landscape. With its own health plan that covers the vast majority of the patients it treats, dedicated distribution and a network of retail pharmacies, Kaiser can completely control drug utilization on its own. This setup also allows Kaiser to block information on this process from reaching manufacturers, rendering much of the analysis recommended in Level 2 segmentation impossible to conduct. There are, however, also opportunities in the closed nature of Kaiser's system. For example, its high level of control over drug usage and integrated record system make Kaiser an excellent partner for the collection of real-world evidence and the evaluation of the economic outcomes of treatment decisions. These unique challenges and opportunities make Kaiser impossible to characterize well using the typical approach.

A second example is an account like UnitedHealth Group, which is often characterized in the same way for different reasons. With UnitedHealth Group's ever-expanding business model, it defies Level 1 categorization because of its continued expansion into new lines of business. Of course, it has its long-established health plan and PBM arms. But with recent acquisitions, including DaVita Medical Group, United has become the single largest employer of physicians in the United States, making it a very formidable provider network as well. This presents a couple of challenges for account segmentation. First, understanding potential becomes far more complex, since it must be considered across multiple business models with some overlap. Second, scale and integration merit coverage considerations that are different from other segmented accounts. Manufacturers are grappling with how to cover UnitedHealth Group—as a payer, provider or something new entirely—and other IPPNs are arguably beginning to achieve the scale that merits special consideration as well. In any case, we see a reason currently to have a separate treatment at least for United, depending on an individual organization's business and whether both payers and providers are influential and being considered for segmentation.

CONCLUDING THOUGHTS

The objective of segmentation is to define "where to play" within the universe of organized customer accounts and to provide segment-level insight for determining "how to win." The multi-level segmentation framework we have introduced (Figure 3.1) addresses two fundamental questions: Which types of account will the organization engage through KAM (Level 1), and how should those accounts be sub-segmented based on addressable potential, control and partnership orientation (Level 2)? Further identification of individual account needs and priorities, and determination of the specific opportunities to target then become the responsibility of the key account manager to determine in accordance with the defined customer engagement process. Once an organization has segmented, selected and tiered its key accounts, the next step is to create a value strategy to drive successful, mutually beneficial partnerships within each segment, tier and account. That's the focus of the next chapter.

CHAPTER FOUR

Value strategy: Evolving from basic offerings to advanced solutions

Joe Stevens, Matt Ruple and Mike Moorman

Developing a clear, compelling and differentiated value strategy is central to the success of any key account management (KAM) program, and KAM programs at life sciences organizations are no exception. Value strategies define the types of customer needs the KAM program will prioritize, and the basic offerings, advanced solutions and associated value propositions that will deliver mutual impact for the customer and the manufacturer.

ZS research reveals that life sciences leaders see the development of advanced solutions that meet their organized customers' higher-order needs as one of the foremost investment priorities for increasing their organization's impact.[1, 2] Without a clear definition of these solutions and their associated value propositions, key account managers have been left to stitch together their own ad hoc value strategies and many have resorted to less-valuable activities, either acting as glorified relationship

DOI: 10.4324/9781003226512-4

managers or focusing narrowly on basic contracting and rebating. Furthermore, in such a highly regulated industry sector, actual and perceived compliance constraints often restrict the extent of value communication and exchange allowed between manufacturers and healthcare providers. These considerations all increase the importance of a carefully designed and executed value strategy.

This chapter defines the critical elements of value strategy and introduces a process for designing and implementing advanced solutions. We emphasize six critical insights:

1. A shared organization-wide understanding of value strategy concepts and associated terminology is an essential first step.
2. Effective advanced solutions and associated value propositions are developed through a customer-centric and comprehensive stepwise approach.
3. Deep customer insight and segmentation are foundational inputs to advanced solutions and value proposition development.
4. Advanced solutions are progressively built, starting with baseline objectives and followed by solution architecture, messaging and proof points.
5. Value strategy and advanced solutions are defined at the segment level, and subsequently tailored to individual customers as part of the customer engagement process (CEP).
6. A dynamic and staged approach to the evolution of advanced solutions can be the fastest path to impact.

A SHARED UNDERSTANDING OF VALUE STRATEGY TERMS AND CONCEPTS IS AN ESSENTIAL FIRST STEP

"Value strategy," "solutions" and "value propositions" are concepts not consistently defined from one organization—or even one person—to the next. This is especially true in life sciences, where business-to-business (B2B) value strategies for organized customers are still new to the industry. An essential first step for any organization aspiring to develop an effective value strategy is to establish a shared understanding of these core concepts. While developing a common language may seem an academic task, many value strategy initiatives have faced major barriers or even failed for lack of a shared understanding of terms and concepts.

Figure 4.1 defines the critical components of "value strategy" as well as the relationship between value strategy and the KAM-led customer engagement process.

Value strategies for key organized customers aren't simply high-level positioning statements or elevator pitches. Rather, they're a combination of objectives, basic offerings, advanced solutions and associated value propositions and messaging defined at the

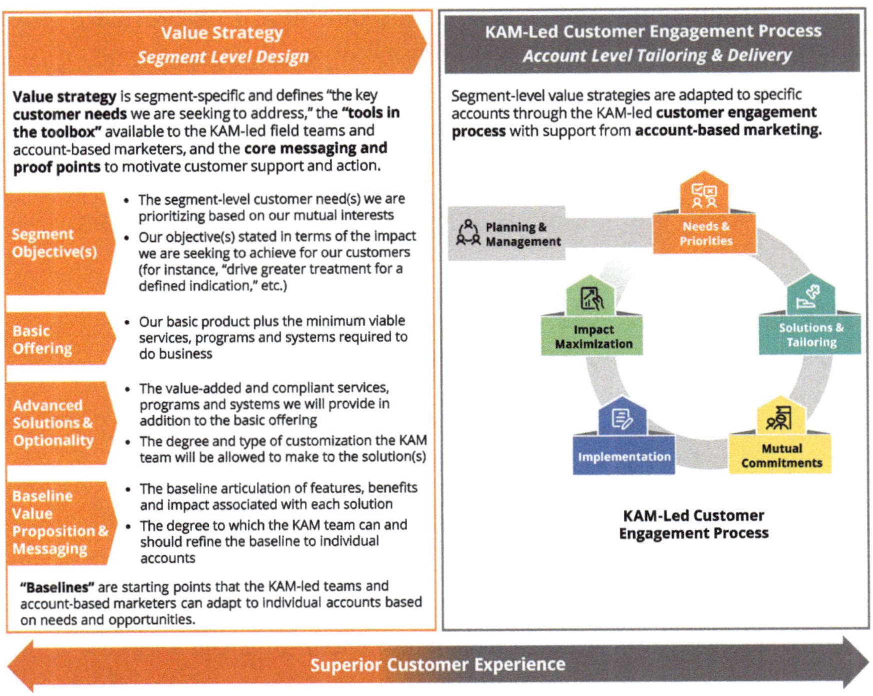

Figure 4.1 *Value strategy components and relationship to customer engagement process.*

segment level. They also clearly specify the degree to which key account managers can customize solutions and value propositions to individual accounts, or "optionality."

A well-defined value strategy ensures that KAM teams have the right tools and direction to effectively and compliantly address customer needs, particularly those needs the company should be best positioned to address. A clear value strategy also provides critical alignment across the key internal functions that must support the key account teams and deliver on the promises these teams make to key organized customers.

Life sciences companies are especially adept at designing and delivering their basic offerings, including not only their core products but also the essential services, programs and systems required for customers to access and use those products. But many life sciences companies at the industry's frontier are now evolving their imperatives from basic offerings to advanced solutions that meet their strategically important organized customers' higher-order needs and that result in greater mutual customer and company benefits. In the remainder of this chapter, we focus on critical success factors and approaches for developing and implementing these advanced solutions.

EFFECTIVE ADVANCED SOLUTIONS ARE DEVELOPED THROUGH A CUSTOMER-CENTRIC AND COMPREHENSIVE STEPWISE APPROACH

For many life sciences organizations, the journey toward advanced solutions has to date been more organic than purposeful. For instance, in many cases, brand teams have developed product-specific offerings and collateral, whereas individual key account managers have been tasked with "co-creating" broader solutions and value propositions. While these managers are admirably attempting to devise new ideas by cobbling together assets, they are often without a well-defined value strategy or clear boundaries for knowing which customer needs or types of solution are within the scope of their assignment. Oftentimes, the solutions implemented are more the function of an account manager's charisma and ability to rally the organization to a particular customer's needs than the result of a comprehensive, well-thought-out strategy. In other cases, an account manager might excite a customer with the promise of new partnership opportunities, only to find that significant internal barriers prevent many of those opportunities from coming to fruition. We shouldn't be surprised when executives begin to question the ROI on these types of unstructured activities.

Developing cohesive and effective advanced solutions for complex B2B organized customers is a relatively new challenge for many life sciences companies. Figure 4.2 provides the stepwise approach that we have found the most effective in meeting this challenge, leading to both the development and execution of advanced solutions.

The design and implementation of advanced solutions is a complex and evolving journey. The stepwise approach described in Figure 4.2 demystifies and simplifies advanced solutions development and continued advancement. Involvement of cross-functional stakeholders at every stage in the process is an important underpinning of this process, and essential to advanced solutions that are supported organizationwide, are differentiated and will drive unique impact for customers, patients and the manufacturer.

In the following sections, we provide an introduction into key aspects of this process.

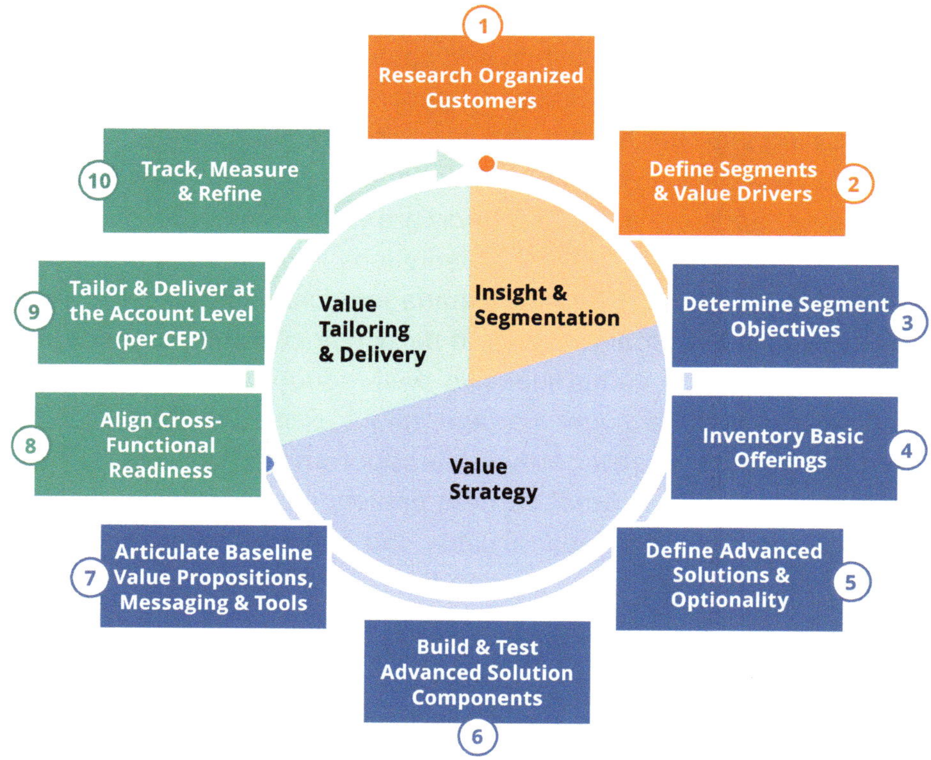

Figure 4.2 *A customer-centric approach to advanced solutions.*

DEEP CUSTOMER INSIGHT AND SEGMENTATION ARE FOUNDATIONAL INPUTS TO ADVANCED SOLUTIONS

Advanced solutions are defined at the segment level and later tailored to individual accounts by key account managers and cross-functional customer-facing team members. As indicated in Figure 4.2, deep insight into the needs and priorities of each organized customer segment selected for KAM is a foundational input to advanced solutions. The best solutions explicitly target the customer needs and priorities that the company is best positioned to address based on company capabilities and mutual interests with each customer segment.

While this customer-centric approach sounds straightforward, it has proven a challenge for many life sciences organizations. One explanation attributes this gap to the different priorities of life sciences manufacturers and their organized customers. Life sciences manufacturers have historically been narrowly focused on the usage of their drugs or devices. Organized customers have a dramatically broader focus and set of priorities, often citing the "triple aim" (improving population health, reducing per capita cost and improving patient experience) or even the "quadruple aim" (which adds employee satisfaction). A particular drug or device occupies only a small fraction of their mindshare, and their priorities extend beyond optimizing usage for one class of product among the thousands they manage every day.

Complicating this issue is that each organized customer is unique in its patient population, geography, management philosophy and positioning in the broader healthcare community. Institutions therefore adopt different priorities from one another, and these priorities inform the different initiatives in which institutions invest. For example, a sophisticated IDN might be focused on system expansion and adding in-house pharmacies, whereas a large group oncology clinic may invest more resources in maximizing drug reimbursement revenue and expanding sites of care across its region.

To most effectively develop advanced solutions, manufacturers should keep in mind the following segmentation principles:

1. Segments should be developed based on a multi-dimensional analysis that considers addressable potential for the life sciences company's products, ability to control or influence usage of those products and willingness to partner or otherwise meaningfully engage with the life sciences company's account management teams.
2. Each segment's underlying needs and priorities should be informed by market research, headquarters-level engagements ("top-to-tops") and KAM team and field insight,

which will become an increasingly significant contributor as KAM matures across life sciences.

3. Segments ought to reflect major differences in customer needs and capabilities, and the number of segments should remain few enough to avoid making execution excessively complex, particularly where KAM teams might be tasked with covering multiple segments. A basic approach may be to distinguish segments based on account type: for instance, one segment might be IDNs, another might be purchasing organizations and a third might be managed care organizations or payers. A more granular approach may involve further sub-segmentation: for example, high-control IDNs might be distinguished from moderate-control IDNs. In some select instances, individual accounts may even be designated as segments unto themselves. Examples in life sciences might include a highly unique "segment of one" such as UnitedHealth Group or a provider such as Kaiser Permanente.

Chapter 3 provides additional insights on segmentation and account selection.

THE COMPONENTS OF ADVANCED SOLUTIONS ARE BUILT PROGRESSIVELY

Designing advanced solutions involves making choices about which of the organized customer's needs to address and which types of solutions will be available to the organization. In this section, we expand on each of the components of value strategy critical to advanced solution development.

SEGMENT OBJECTIVES

Segment objectives provide the "north star" for guiding the life sciences company toward the specific customer needs it has

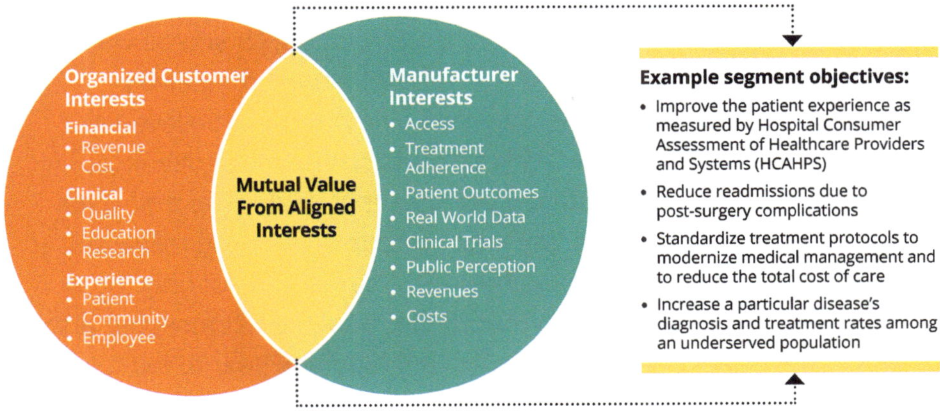

Figure 4.3 *Examples of segment objectives derived from mutual interests.*

chosen to prioritize. Segment objectives directly impact the types of advanced solutions and baseline value propositions the company then develops, and foster clarity and consistency throughout the organization on direction and intent.

As illustrated in Figure 4.3, segment objectives for advanced solutions are determined by identifying areas of mutual interest between the manufacturer and a given segment of its organized customers.

A truism for KAM is that it's relatively easy to identify ways to create value for customers, but much harder to identify ways that benefit both organizations. By focusing on areas of mutual interest, the manufacturer helps to ensure that the advanced solutions it proposes will result in mutual benefits for both parties.

To identify the most attractive areas of mutual interest between an organization and one of its segments, organizations should consider the following questions:

1. Which of the segment's key value drivers, needs and priorities is the organization capable of addressing?
2. How would the organization addressing these value drivers, needs and priorities result in benefits to the customer, to patients and to the organization?

For example, one life sciences company decided that its objective for a particular segment characterized by low CMS scores was to “reduce readmission rates” for patients who had received acute care in a specific therapy area. The company believed it could leverage the unique efficacy of its current drug offerings, in addition to potential advanced services that could help a hospital avoid the need to readmit patients by better managing follow-up care in an outpatient setting. The result benefitted not only the hospital’s patients, who achieved better health outcomes, but also the hospital’s finances, since hospitals regularly bear at least part of the cost of readmissions.

As a consequence of this segment objective, the life sciences company then developed advanced solutions comprised of training, behavioral change management services and a process to share tips and best practices. The baseline value proposition and proof points the company built around these solutions emphasized “better outcomes and increased financial solvency through improvement in quality measures tied to reimbursement.”

EVOLVING FROM BASIC OFFERINGS TO ADVANCED SOLUTIONS

Developing and implementing the basic offering is a strength for most life sciences companies, whereas advanced solutions are a work in progress. Advanced solutions define two things: (1) the services, programs and systems that will be available from the company in addition to the basic offering; and (2) the optionality that KAM teams will have at their disposal for customizing those services, programs and systems to individual accounts. Over time, companies will develop and continually refine a portfolio of advanced solutions as customer needs and value strategy objectives also evolve.

Advanced solutions can be thought of as “wrap-arounds” to the basic offering, as illustrated in Figure 4.4.

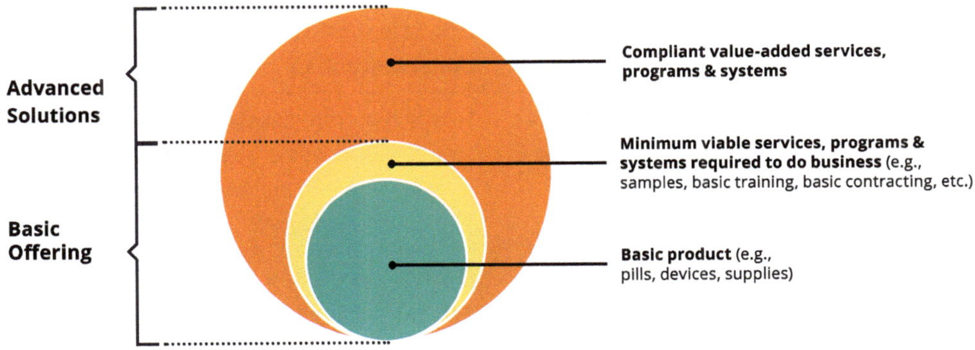

Figure 4.4 *Basic offering versus advanced solutions.*

Many life sciences companies have already begun to identify and implement innovative advanced solutions with strategically important organized customers. Figure 4.5 provides some examples of these solutions.

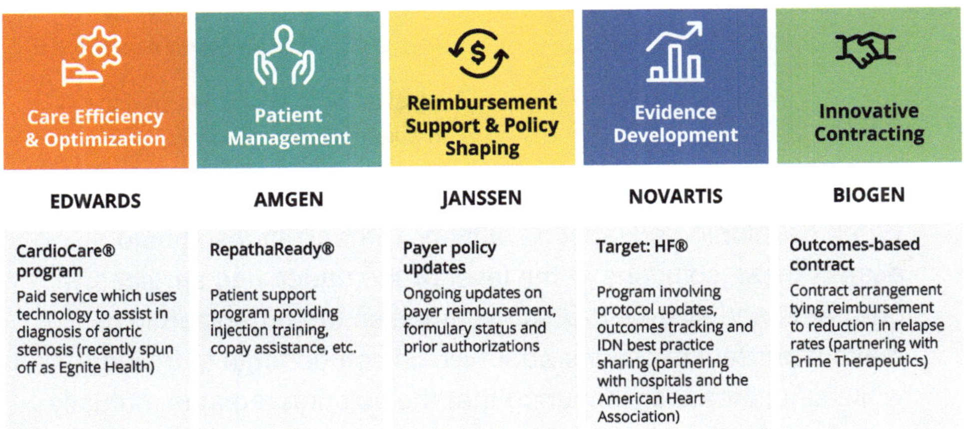

Figure 4.5 *Life sciences examples of advanced solutions (public sources).*
Sources: https://www.cardiocareconnect.com/; https://egnitehealth.com/; https://www.repatha.com/-repathaready-services; https://www.janssencarepath.com/hcp/invega-trinza/insurance-coverage; https://www.heart.org/en/professional/quality-improvement/target-heart-failure; https://www.primetherapeutics.com/en/news/pressreleases/2017/ms-care-centered-contract-release.html

A life sciences organization might entertain many types of advanced solutions. Navigating the extensive possibilities requires systematically considering several critical factors, including the following:

Customer Considerations	Life Sciences Company Considerations
1. To what degree does the customer likely value the advanced solution in relation to its key priorities? 2. What investments and other commitments will the advanced solution require the customer to make? 3. How long will it take until the customer realizes benefits? 4. What barriers to gaining internal agreement and support is the customer likely to face?	1. Which current assets and capabilities would be leveraged to develop and implement the advanced solution? 2. Which partners, if any, would be required? 3. At what cost can the organization develop and deliver the advanced solution? 4. How differentiated is the advanced solution in the marketplace? 5. How much value will the advanced solution provide to the organization? 6. When would value be realized and what is the solution's overall feasibility? 7. What safeguards are required to ensure compliance?

When developing advanced solutions, organizations should assess these solutions at the level of the underlying services, programs and systems. Doing so enables the organization to make important decisions about which components to include while simultaneously ensuring that the solution remains mutually beneficial for the organization and its customers. For instance, an advanced solutions design team might determine that an in-person consultant service would be too expensive to deliver or would create compliance challenges, but that an interactive web-based solution strikes a good balance for both the customer and the company. In this case, the organization should prefer the latter to include as a component of the overall advanced solution.

The degree to which a KAM team will be afforded optionality to customize solutions for individual customers is a critical strategy decision for any organization. A high degree of optionality increases the potential value to the customer, but also increases execution costs, complexity and risk for the organization offering the solution.

Optionality fundamentally spans three levels, ranging from no customization to high customization.

1. No optionality: All customers receive the same solution.
2. Menu optionality: The company offers a menu of options for some or all elements of each advanced solution from which key account managers can then tailor customer-specific solutions.
3. Bespoke optionality: Key account managers are enabled to co-create innovative, bespoke, one-off solutions for a given customer.

Decisions about which components to include in advanced solutions, and what amount of optionality to allow, have ramifications that will be felt throughout the entire organization. It's therefore vital that an advanced solutions development team include cross-functional leaders, and that members with either a non-commercial (for instance, medical) focus or a complementary expertise (for instance, technology or digital health) be brought aboard to collaborate with the KAM team and with marketers. While the team's exact composition can vary by company according to need, diversity ensures the team reflects the best possible insight into customer needs and company capabilities and economics. A cross-functional advanced solution design team will also serve to best educate the key internal stakeholders who must both "sell" and then "deliver" the solution, and will ensure these stakeholders are committed to the solution and well-aligned with its aims. Account managers who can be certain the company is fully supportive of KAM and its solutions will be far more confident and capable of generating customer interest and commitment. Advanced solutions that have strong cross-functional support from the outset are also far more likely to result in successful implementation and mutual benefit.

BASELINE VALUE PROPOSITIONS AND MESSAGING FOR ADVANCED SOLUTIONS

The customer's buy-in to any advanced solution will ultimately depend on their belief in that solution's value relative to costs and potential risks. A manufacturer can achieve that understanding with customers through a compelling value proposition. But it's critical for organizations to recognize that the value proposition is not the solution itself. Rather, the value proposition is an articulation of the benefits and outcomes the advanced solution is expected to generate for the customer. The value proposition messaging typically needs to be articulated differently for different stakeholders within the customer organization based on their respective roles and associated priorities.

Ultimately, the only value that matters is that which is "understood and agreed" by the customer. For this reason, the most compelling value propositions are those that fully illuminate the benefits the customer will realize in relation to their most pressing needs and priorities, and that are quantified based on objective data and supported by compelling proof points.

A best practice is to develop "baseline" value propositions as starting points from which the KAM team can then tailor to individual accounts and decision makers during the customer engagement process. In many cases, customers themselves might help to establish the business value based on their own internal knowledge and data. In these cases, the value proposition is jointly developed by the KAM team and the customer. Customer inaction is often the chief obstacle the KAM team is trying to overcome, and why a compelling value proposition the customer deeply understands, believes in and cares about is critical.

CUSTOMER ENGAGEMENT LED BY KAM TRANSLATES SEGMENT-LEVEL ADVANCED SOLUTIONS TO THE INDIVIDUAL ACCOUNT LEVEL

While segments are designed to capture customers or organizations that share certain characteristics, each account is invariably unique, and a big question in KAM is how to ensure that advanced solutions address these individual accounts' particular circumstances. The answer is the KAM-led customer engagement process (CEP).

The CEP is the means by which an organization more fully understands and confirms an individual account's needs and priorities, and by which the organization can then identify, tailor and implement the right advanced solutions for the account. Figure 4.6 provides a high-level example of a CEP for key accounts.

For solutions that allow a high degree of optionality, the CEP ensures the customer is deeply involved in the tailoring process in ways that maximize the customer's understanding of the value and that builds their commitment to moving forward. And even where the value strategy calls for a standardized solution with no optionality, the CEP still helps to ensure customer centricity. Collaborating with customers to identify and confirm needs before proposing an advanced solution ensures the value proposition and the solution can be explicitly positioned to meet the customer's specifically articulated priorities.

The CEP provides a clear roadmap and role clarity for all the functions responsible for ensuring successful solution tailoring,

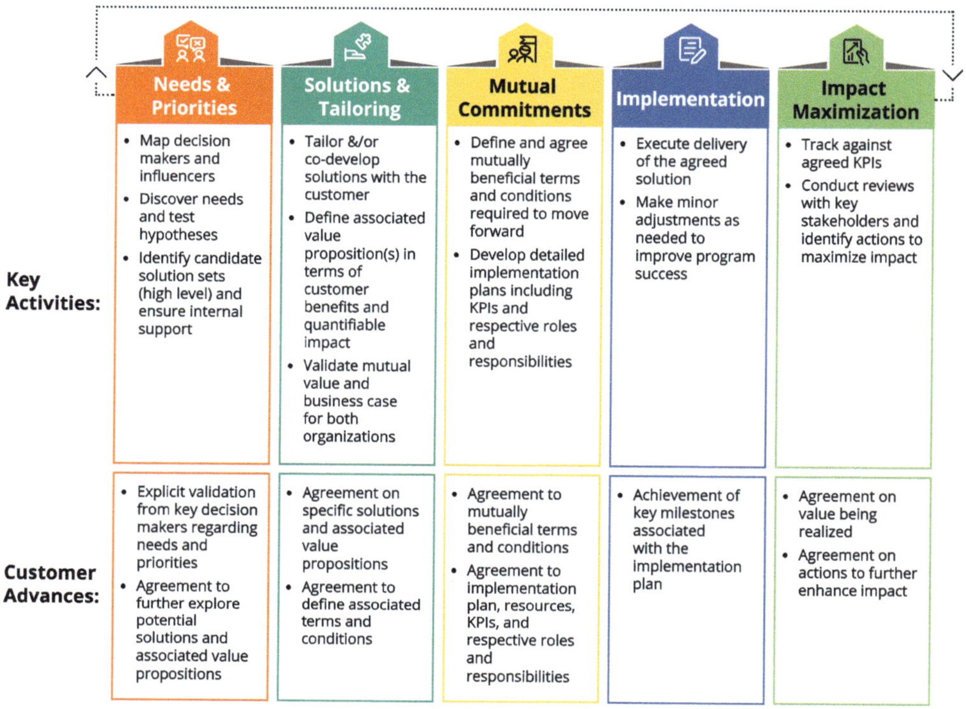

Figure 4.6 *Example customer engagement process (CEP).*

implementation and pull-through. It also helps the KAM team close the loop with customers—aiding them in understanding the value being achieved and proactively identifying any lingering shortfalls or upside opportunities. Well-executed CEPs are the path to a differentiated and superior customer experience. We discuss more about the CEP in Chapter 9.

TO ADVANCE YOUR B2B VALUE STRATEGY, TAKE IT ONE STEP AT A TIME

The capacity to design unique and mutually beneficial B2B value strategies and advanced solutions for complex and increasingly important organized customers is an emerging innovation in life sciences. Most life sciences leaders recognize that more effective advanced solutions are a major priority for their KAM programs and for continued success with organized customers more broadly.

Developing advanced solutions and organizational capabilities is a journey. For many life sciences companies, a closed-loop development process and a "walk, jog, run" approach will likely lead to the fastest results with the least business risk. In our experience, three actions are key:

1. Create an inventory of current assets and find ways to better integrate and align those capabilities against specific customer needs, as well as to better communicate, prove and reinforce the value proposition. Many life sciences companies already provide at least some advanced solutions to their customers, often in fragmented ways, without receiving any recognition for the unique value they're creating. This is low-hanging fruit.
2. Don't assume new advanced solutions have to be "home runs." Instead, start with smaller solutions the customer can more easily understand and adopt. Build trust and confidence, then move to more ambitious solutions.
3. Use "early experience teams" (EET™s) (see Chapter 9) and dynamic processes to rapidly test and refine new advanced solutions with a small set of well-selected accounts. The learnings from these EETs will pay big dividends in ensuring good solutions and proof points while simultaneously building organizational capabilities.

CONCLUDING THOUGHTS

"Customer centricity," "co-creation" and "partnering" are the words organizations often use to describe their reasons for pursuing KAM as an overall business strategy. However, without a compelling value strategy, these words ring hollow. Most life sciences companies recognize that a more structured and compelling approach to advanced solutions is one of their top priorities. At the same time, organized customers are becoming increasingly willing to partner with manufacturers to address their most pressing needs.[3] Taking a systematic and staged approach to advanced solutions design, validation and rollout will accelerate success for all parties.

NOTES

1 ZS and Strategic Account Management Association, "State of Key Account Management in Pharma" and "State of Key Account Management in Medtech," Q4 2020.

2 "Organized customers" are defined as healthcare-related companies with a professional, dedicated management structure such as managed care organizations (MCOs), integrated delivery networks (IDNs) and large dialysis organizations (LDOs). The term is used to differentiate from solo or group physician practices where management decisions are usually made by physicians or other staff members whose primary focus is on patient care.

3 ZS, "Provider Organization Partnership Tracker Wave 3" study, November 2020.

CHAPTER FIVE

KAM organization design: Form follows function

Mike Moorman and Jude Konzelmann

The rise of the "organized customer" has brought key account management (KAM) to the forefront in the pharmaceutical and medtech industries. As IDNs, IPPNs, national payers, regional payers, group practices and other account types consolidate, increase control and assume risk, KAM will continue to gain importance.

While KAM is becoming an industry priority, the shape KAM will take from one company to the next will be unique. KAM is an organization-wide business strategy, not just a role. There are many ways in which pharmaceutical and medtech companies may organize to create new and innovative value for large organized customers. The right organization design will depend on the customer experience and types of value the KAM program is intended to create, and the types of benefits the life sciences company wants in return.

DOI: 10.4324/9781003226512-5

In this chapter, we provide insights related to four fundamental KAM models, broader organization design considerations and emerging trends. We draw upon experience across a large cross-section of B2B industries with a focus on unique aspects of the pharmaceutical and medtech industries.

INSIGHT NO. 1: FORM FOLLOWS FUNCTION

It's hard to argue with the wisdom of the adage, "If you don't know where you're going, any road will get you there." In the context of KAM models and organization design, this concept translates into "form follows function."

Before a company can achieve the optimal KAM model and organization design, leadership must first determine function. This means understanding what customer needs, priorities and experience the company wants to address by pursuing a KAM strategy, what types of offerings and solutions this implies and what benefits the company gets in return.

When defining function, identifying possible ways to create customer value is easy. The list is endless. What's hard is identifying ways to create customer value and an associated customer experience that will result in commensurate benefits for the company.

"Mutual value" is the name of the game and the only way to justify KAM. Figuring out which types of mutual value life sciences companies should pursue—and how—is a value strategy question (Figure 5.1).

The types of solutions, value and experience the KAM organization is meant to develop, tailor and deliver influence a host of organization design drivers, including the:

- Decision influencers at the organized customer who will need to be engaged and to what end

- Mix of customer-facing roles and skills that will be required to achieve this engagement
- Level of coordination and collaboration that will be required between customer-facing roles and internal functions
- Type of cross-functional support the customer-facing teams will need at each stage in the customer decision journey

In the rush to KAM, many life sciences companies have inadvertently glossed over their value strategy. They have picked up on themes like "co-creation" and "customer centricity," while remaining relatively ambiguous about the types of value and solutions they envisioned. In some cases, the result has been a type of KAM "faith-walk," with value strategy being thrown over the fence to the field to try to figure out.

Best-practice companies think through their value strategy and potential offerings as a first step, not an afterthought (see

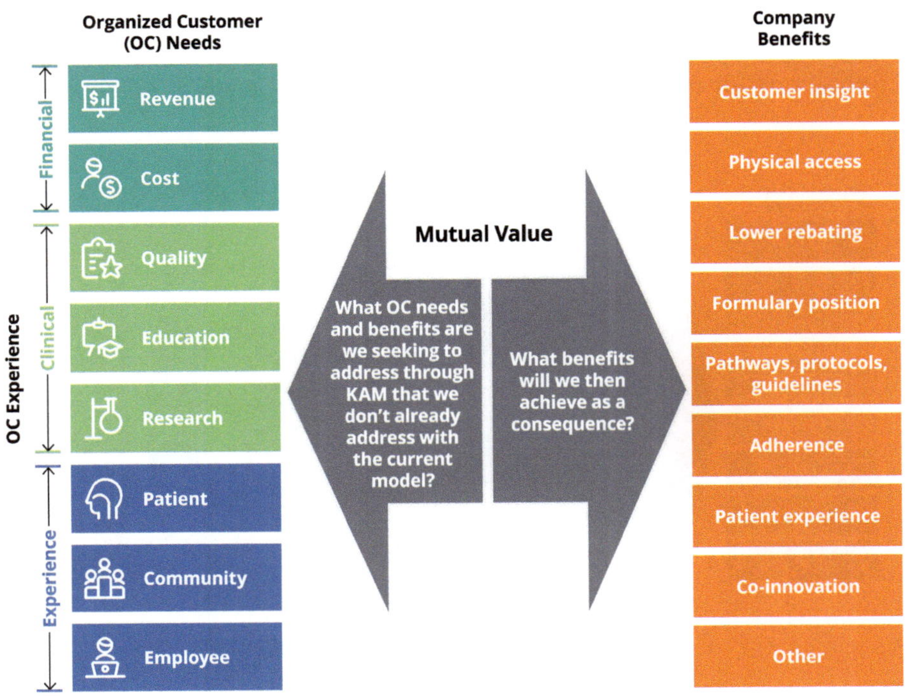

Figure 5.1 *Potential sources of mutual value.*

Chapter 4 for a detailed discussion on value strategy). That doesn't mean they have all the answers, but they at least have strong hypotheses with a reasonable degree of confidence. They start with a strong vision for "function" and then move to "form."

INSIGHT NO. 2: ONE SIZE DOESN'T FIT ALL

Fundamentally, life sciences companies might employ four account management models. Type 3 and Type 4 models are clearly considered KAM. Type 2 is entry-level KAM. Type 1 is basic account management (AM) (Figure 5.2).

No one model is inherently better or worse than the others. All four types of account management have a time and place. The right model is situational and is a function of the organization's objectives. For instance, Type 3 KAM is better if the strategy is cost-effective scalability and tight control on solution types and messaging. Type 4 KAM is better if the goal is one-off bespoke solutions for unique customers willing to invest in such solutions.

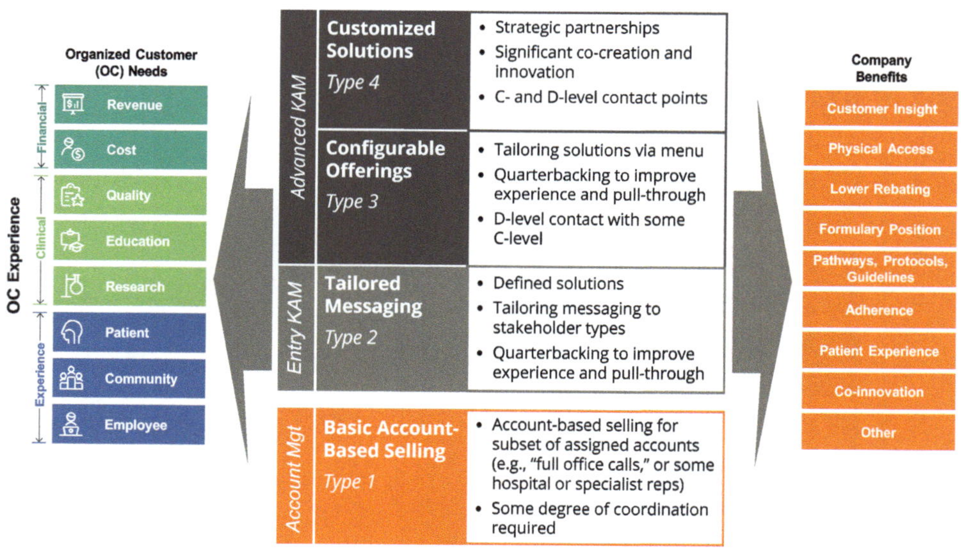

Figure 5.2 *Fundamental KAM and AM models.*

The customer engagement processes, competencies, internal business processes and support required for each of the KAM models is quite different. The choice of model depends on the intended strategy and expected business impact.

Furthermore, the four account management models are not mutually exclusive. In fact, it's more common than not for companies to employ some or all in combination. For instance, some companies use Type 4 KAM for a small subset of prominent strategic customers that value and reward true co-creation, and employ Type 3 KAM for the next tier of large, high-control key accounts. They then use Type 2 KAM for large individual facilities (which can be part of a Type 3 or Type 4 customer or can be stand-alone) and reserve Type 1 AM for mid-sized stand-alone customers or locations that are part of a larger customer engaged through Type 2 KAM, Type 3 KAM or Type 4 KAM.

The determination of the right combination and deployment of models depends on trade-offs between effectiveness, efficiency, agility and feasibility.

For key accounts, most life sciences companies currently operate in the range of Type 2 KAM to Type 3 KAM and aspire to evolve to Type 3 to Type 4 KAM. KAM is a journey and the competencies and organizational capabilities required to execute at higher levels take time and focused investment to build. The customer also must be ready and able to work in these new ways.

INSIGHT NO. 3: KAM IS AN ORGANIZATION-WIDE MODEL, NOT A ROLE

The focus for KAM organization design is sometimes over-indexed to the key account manager role. No doubt the design of that role is mission critical. But organization design for KAM goes well beyond the key account manager. Take, for instance, the

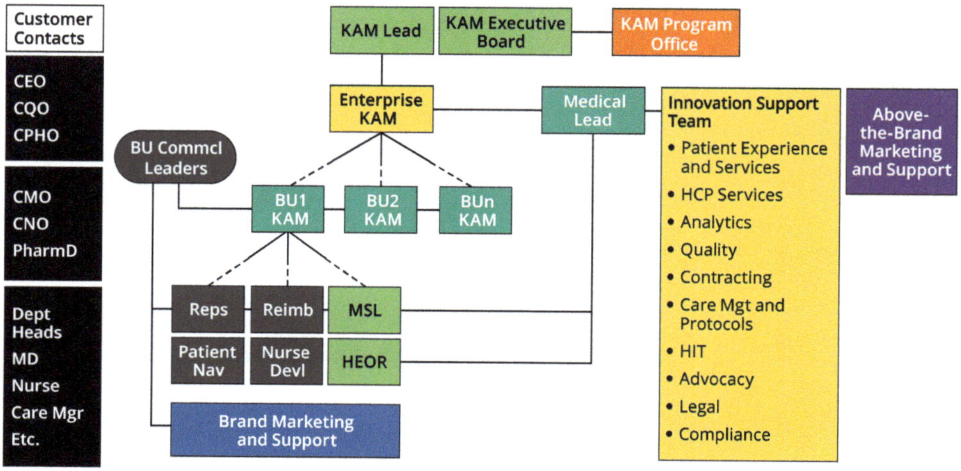

Figure 5.3 *Cross-functional organization design for KAM.*

organization design for a hypothetical pharmaceutical company as depicted in Figure 5.3.

While this is just an illustrative example, it highlights a host of organization design questions typical of KAM. As summarized in Figure 5.4, these include decisions related to roles design, reporting relationships, sizing, deployment and cross-functional support.

These obviously are complex questions that touch many leaders and parts of the organization. KAM is an organization-wide business strategy, not a role. Determining the optimal organization design requires a rigorous assessment of effectiveness, efficiency, agility, disruption and execution risks. Frequently, the ideal organization design may need to be reached in stages. For instance, for newer KAM programs, the best practice is to start small and scale over time.

CONCLUDING THOUGHTS

Many life sciences companies are still in the relatively early phases of their KAM journey. This shouldn't be a surprise. Even

KAM Organization Design Decisions

What types of account management models should we have (Type 1 through 4) and where?

Should we have both business unit KAMs and enterprise KAMs, and if so, in what combinations?

Where should each of our KAM roles report (such as KAM leadership, sales leadership, market access leadership and others)?

Which key decision influencers will each of the KAM roles engage relative to other customer-facing roles? Where there is overlap, what are the relative roles and responsibilities?

How many KAMs of each type is optimal? How should they be deployed?

What customer-facing field roles or internal roles should be designated as the "core account team" versus the "extended account team"? What does that designation imply and what is the reporting relationship to the KAM (for example, dotted line, solid line or none)?

In what situations should core team roles be dedicated to a given key account or group of key accounts? If not dedicated, how can core team roles be deployed to best facilitate account team cohesiveness and collaboration?

What internal supporting functions are required and how should they be structured and resourced (for example, above-the-brand marketing, solutions support team or implementation support team)?

What should be the responsibilities of the KAM program office or center of excellence? Which roles within the program office should be dedicated versus a shared resource with other functions? Where should the KAM program office or CoE report?

Should a formal executive board be formed to oversee the KAM program strategy, objectives and organizational alignment? Who should sit on the board and what's the operating model?

Figure 5.4 *Typical organization design questions.*

KAM pioneers, such as IBM, Schneider Electric and other KAM "all-stars," are still working to improve their KAM programs. These companies started their KAM journey in the late 1980s, decades before most life sciences companies.

As the life sciences industry continues to innovate and advance KAM strategies for organized customers, we should expect to see new and novel models emerge. A dynamic customer environment will fuel this change.

Healthcare systems are evolving at both the local and national levels. Vertical integration has led to mega-payers that now represent a whole new type of customer entity and opportunity. Integration in the IDN and IPPN space, coupled with increased control and risk assumption, is driving the same on the provider side. Pharmaceutical and medtech companies will have to evolve in response to these changes. Anticipating and getting ahead of the change would be better still.

In fact, innovative and agile next-generation KAM strategies are already emerging in life sciences. For example, an explosion in data is allowing both pharmaceutical and medtech companies to unlock whole new approaches to organized customer insight, assessment and micro-segmentation. The next phase in account segmentation will allow for even more targeted and tailored KAM strategies and programs.

A number of organizations are beginning to advance to KAM models that are highly customized to individual key accounts. Some are taking this a full step further: developing go-to-market models that are customized to unique local healthcare markets (LHMs). These LHM-specific strategies address all aspects of market coverage and customer engagement, including customized KAM models.

Leading-edge dynamic analytical models are starting to allow for local and account-level resource mix and deployment optimization in real-time using opportunity derived from patient flow information. These models promise to significantly increase agility and support patient-centric strategies.

Finally, new types of solution and go-to-market partnerships are being formed with third-party companies. The goal is to provide innovative solutions beyond the pill and beyond the box.

The future is bright for KAM, and in many ways, the future is now.

CHAPTER SIX

Executive alignment and engagement: It's make or break for life sciences KAM programs

Mike Moorman and Namita Powers

When it comes to the success of a key account management (KAM) program, it's difficult to overstate the importance of alignment and active engagement from the senior-most executive team. Because KAM is an organization-wide business strategy, not a role or a sales-only initiative, internal barriers can conspire to dramatically undermine the success of nearly any KAM program—and thereby the company's success with strategically important customers. These barriers can include internal silos, insufficient investment and resources, conflicting internal priorities, an inability to attract the best talent and short-term time horizons.

Strong executive understanding, alignment, engagement and support play a critical role in overcoming these barriers and

DOI: 10.4324/9781003226512-6

sustaining the execution and commitment required to foster strategic partnerships and impact. Executive engagement also improves access to the customer's senior-most executives and is vital to the success of the broader program.

Companies can achieve the level and type of executive alignment and engagement required for KAM by focusing on five key approaches, as illustrated in Figure 6.1.

Together, these five approaches ensure that the executive team:

- Builds a deep understanding of KAM
- Is fully bought into the strategy and time horizons
- Assumes co-accountability for success
- Drives the required operating model throughout the organization
- Personally supports select accounts

In the remainder of this chapter, we explore in more detail each of these five approaches for achieving executive alignment and engagement.

Figure 6.1 *Best-practice approaches for executive alignment and active engagement.*

THE EXECUTIVE TEAM MUST CO-OWN THE KAM STRATEGY FOR IT TO SUCCEED

KAM in life sciences is a strategy focused on providing unique offerings and value through an orchestrated, cross-functional, go-to-market model designed specifically to address the needs and engagement preferences of a defined segment of large, complex and strategically important systems and groups. KAM is dramatically different from the brand-centric and doctor-focused one-to-one engagement models that have served life sciences so well for many years and that will continue to be important in segments of the market. KAM is a many-to-many B2B engagement model and requires life sciences organizations to work in new ways across their customer-facing roles and within internal functions. Creating new internal support functions and reengineering cross-functional operating models and metrics are part of the KAM equation.

As with any organization-wide business strategy, a deep level of senior executive engagement in formulating the vision, business case and design is imperative. We've seen many life sciences organizations approach KAM narrowly as a "role" or as a "sales initiative." Such approaches are typically born from a lack of understanding of KAM and often receive lighter senior executive engagement. The result can be a watered-down version of KAM, varying senior executive commitment, an incomplete and inconsistent understanding of the strategy and cross-functional requirements, and unclear success metrics.

Deep involvement of the senior executive team in the KAM strategy formulation and success metrics is essential. Counter to most B2B industries, many senior executives in life sciences came up through their organizations at a time when KAM was not yet a common or important business strategy. As a result, many of these executives lack significant experience in KAM and don't have a deep understanding of its purposes and advantages. Engagement in the KAM vision, business case and design provides a pivotal opportunity to fully immerse executive leadership in ways that ensure the right KAM strategy and resources are in place while simultaneously building KAM fluency and conviction.

The following are aspects of KAM strategy we've found require special attention from senior executives:

1. Segmentation and account selection
2. Value strategy
3. Organization design
4. Operating model
5. Metrics and motivation systems

The first four of these areas have substantial implications for broader organization design, ways of working and investments. The fifth area, metrics and motivation systems, ensures a shared vision and understanding for "what success will look like," including near-term and longer-term expectations. KAM programs that fail to achieve a shared understanding of success metrics and time horizons invariably fall victim to near-term transactional priorities and pressures.

KAM EXECUTIVE BOARDS HELP TO ENSURE CO-ACCOUNTABILITY AT THE LEVEL WHERE IT MATTERS

Driving organization-wide understanding and execution of the KAM strategy requires engagement from the entire executive team. Executive teams that place sole ownership of the KAM strategy and results on the shoulders of the KAM program leader are setting the organization up for poor results.

KAM is a cross-functional team sport. It requires strong coordination between key account managers and many other customer-facing roles, each of which report into different parts of the organization. Similarly, KAM needs support from functions like marketing, human resources, training, analytics, legal and compliance, and others that also have separate leadership and reporting structures. And in many cases, KAM can require the orchestration of functions and roles across business units (BUs), which again have their own leadership structures. Assuming the KAM program leader can motivate the alignment of resources and priorities across this matrix is unrealistic, yet not uncommon. Significant senior executive engagement and accountability is required to drive such organization-wide alignment.

The formation of a "KAM Executive Board" is one approach that some leading-practice organizations have employed to ensure organization-wide alignment to the KAM strategy. This board shares responsibility with the KAM program leader for the following aspects of annual strategy, planning and execution:

- Setting KAM strategy and objectives (including annual or longer-term targets)
- Determining and agreeing on resource requirements and commitments
- Ensuring execution of the agreed-upon strategy, resources and prioritization within their respective businesses, functions and regions
- Co-owning accountability for business results

Strategies and programs owned and advocated by senior-most executives get attention. The KAM Executive Board aligns executives to the KAM strategy while ensuring the executive engagement and accountability necessary to drive alignment and execution within their individual functions, businesses or regions.

The composition of KAM Executive Boards isn't uniform across companies. Form must follow function and be geared toward addressing the internal silos that will most affect the KAM program's success. Take, for example, the following alternative board compositions, each of which addresses different types of silos:

- **Enterprise and BU leaders board:** President, the KAM program leader, and general managers or chief commercial officers from each of the BUs most affected by KAM
- **Functional leaders board:** President, the KAM program leader, and senior leaders of each of the functions that must collaborate to achieve KAM excellence (including KAM, sales, medical, marketing, human resources, training, analytics, finance, legal or compliance)
- **Hybrid board:** A hybrid approach comprising a mix of enterprise, BU or functional leaders, with board composition that is small enough to be effective

Note that in some cases the KAM Executive Board's responsibilities might be incorporated into the charter and accountabilities of an existing Executive Leadership Team (ELT) rather than be tasked to a newly formed board. In these cases, it is key to ensure that KAM receives sufficient focus and accountability from the ELT relative to their many other priorities and agenda items.

EXECUTIVE COMMUNICATIONS MUST DEMONSTRATE UNITY AND CONVICTION

KAM is a relatively new strategy for much of life sciences and is not necessarily well-understood by all leaders, managers and teams. Building an organization-wide understanding and commitment to the company's KAM strategy, rationale, roadmap, expectations and proof points requires systematic, consistent and repeated executive communication, coupled with visible role-modeling. These responsibilities cannot be left solely to the KAM program leader.

Executives must consistently position KAM as a strategic priority that maximizes impact with critically important and unique organized customers. Emphasizing the organization-wide implications and expectations required for KAM is another communication imperative.

When senior executive communications fall short, a number of tell-tale signs emerge. These include:

- A high degree of internal confusion regarding KAM's intent and the role of individual key account managers
- Leaders and managers within the organization who describe the KAM strategy and intent differently from one another
- KAM program leaders who find themselves needing to invest inordinate time in internal "road shows" to try to explain and sell the KAM strategy and vision
- Destructive and unnecessary consternation regarding the importance of KAM versus the traditional sales organization
- Top talent who are reluctant to assume KAM-related roles for fear the strategy is unclear or the organization isn't committed to the program

Effective executive communication creates clarity and motivates the organization and individuals to action. While the nature and content of executive communications obviously evolve as the KAM program matures, some common success factors are critical to achieve at any stage:

- **Clarity:** Clarity around key communication points relating to strategy, rationale, stakeholder benefits, roadmap and expectations that results in organization-wide understanding and motivation
- **Consistency:** Consistency in the communications by all senior executives that results in a common understanding and that demonstrates executive alignment and conviction
- **Inclusion:** Balanced communications that appropriately reinforce the continued importance of existing functions

(including sales) to mitigate perceived threats and cross-functional conflict

- **Relevancy:** Practices and enablers that ensure clarity, consistency and audience relevancy as messaging filters down through the ranks and convey "what this means for me"
- **Reinforcement and proof points:** Reinforcement by senior executives accompanied by compelling proof points that keeps KAM a front-and-center priority and drives continuous improvement in organization-wide execution

Clear, consistent, inclusive, relevant and reinforced executive communication plays an enormous role in driving the organization-wide understanding and motivation required for KAM. It's also worth noting that the very act of preparing for and delivering such communications helps ensure top executives are themselves fully aligned with and supportive of the KAM strategy and the associated requirements for their respective businesses, functions and regions.

EXECUTIVE SPONSORSHIP PROGRAMS CAN BE A GAME-CHANGER WHEN DONE WELL

Executive Sponsorship Programs (ESPs) that directly engage select executives as dedicated members of individual account teams can be a powerful way to increase impact with strategically critical customers. The broader KAM program can also benefit from ESPs. In-the-trenches engagement can provide executives with insights and experience that result in stronger KAM advocacy with their peers and with the broader organization. However, ESPs are a double-edged sword. Poorly designed and executed ESPs have been noted as a source of more damage than benefit. Therefore, ESPs must be rigorously designed and executed to achieve positive impact while mitigating risks.

Before going deeper into ESPs, it's beneficial to confirm what ESPs aren't: "sounding boards," "steering committees," "occasional touch-bases with the customer" or other forms of light senior executive involvement. Having the executive "take control" of the team or the account is also neither the intent nor desired. Unfortunately, there are endless stories of ESPs and executive engagement with customers gone bad.

Some common themes include executives who:

- Go off-message during critical customer meetings
- Make customer commitments the organization can't keep
- Agree hastily to something not in the company's best interest
- Undermine the key account manager's authority and future impact
- Damage relationships by creating a poor customer experience

Executives are highly capable individuals, and these outcomes are less a reflection on talent and more on poor ESP design and mismatches between capacity, expectations and fit.

Conversely, well-designed and executed ESPs deliver substantial benefits, not the least of which include:

- Greater access to and deeper relationships with important customer executives
- Increased ability to align and ensure internal resources as necessary to maximize impact with a key account
- Improved executive acumen during strategy planning and customer interactions, and focused apprenticeship in this competency for the associated key account manager and other team members on the account
- More-informed advocacy for KAM by executive sponsors with their peers and other key internal stakeholders as a result of their hands-on experience and insights

- Better executive-level understanding of KAM impact, success metrics and realistic timeframes
- Greater executive appreciation and support for eliminating internal barriers and further advancing the organization-wide operating model

As depicted in Figure 6.2, a well-designed ESP gets the right executives with the right profiles and capacity working in the right ways with the right accounts.

Executive sponsors are a hands-on member of the key account team. They work in partnership with the key account manager in accordance with the broader account strategy and plan. They're as willing to follow as they are to lead and apprentice. And they're prepared to make the time commitment necessary to execute their role at each stage of the customer engagement process (CEP). Typically, this involves more of their time during the needs and solutioning, internal resources alignment and value readout and maximization phases of the engagement process. But executive sponsors should also be prepared to step in to help address internal barriers that emerge during implementation and other phases of the CEP as well.

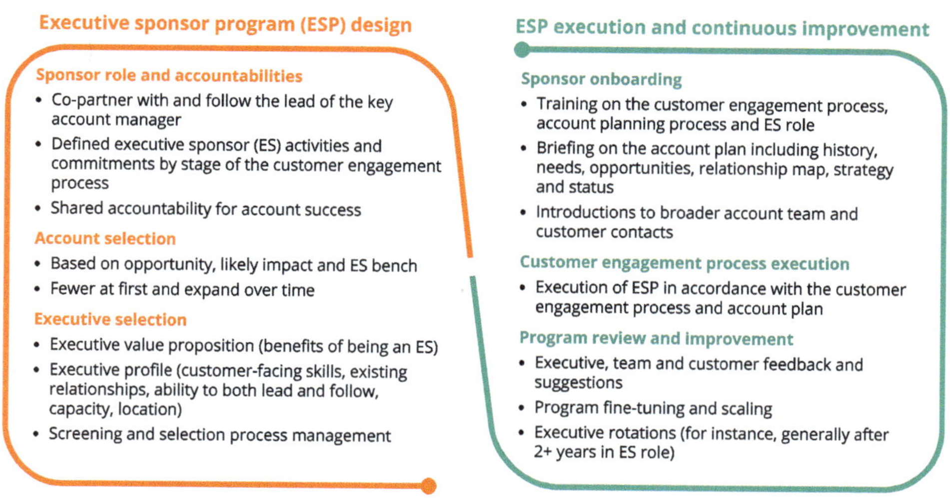

Figure 6.2 *Achieving a highly effective Executive Sponsorship Program.*

A well-executed ESP includes executive sponsor on-boarding and expectations setting, rigorous preparation before customer interactions, post-meeting follow-ups and continuous improvement. Executive sponsors must be deeply versed in the CEP and their role relative to that of other team members and functions. They must also become deeply versed in the account situation, strategy and players. Planning processes to ensure the executive is fully prepared for every client interaction are mission critical. Post-call debriefs and action planning are equally as important.

ESPs typically start off with a fewer number of accounts and executives to allow for hyper-attention to program design and support. They focus on high-opportunity accounts that are the most ready for ESP and on executives who fit the right profile and are the most passionate about the opportunity. Over time, the program can scale while also recognizing that embedding an executive sponsor in an account is a strategic decision, and that not all key accounts will necessarily warrant this level of resource commitment and prioritization.

The degree to which executives seek out and even compete for opportunities to assume an executive sponsor role speaks volumes about an organization's culture and its commitment to customer-centricity. The executive sponsor role is one of the few ways in which executives can remain deeply connected with customers and with their evolving needs and engagement preferences. Just as important, the sponsor role provides executives with an opportunity to directly affect one or several of the organization's most strategic customers.

TOP-TO-TOP MEETINGS SHOULD BE DONE RIGHT OR NOT AT ALL

"Top-to-tops" are strategic planning meetings that bring together customer and supplier executives to understand mutual objectives and priorities, and to identify potential ways to partner moving forward. For accounts with an executive sponsor, top-to-tops are a defined and systematically managed aspect of the overall CEP. However, top-to-tops can also be used for key accounts that aren't formally included in the Executive Sponsorship Program, and in some cases might be a precursor to implementing an ESP with a given account.

Much like ESPs, there are stories of both great success and great failure associated with good and bad top-to-tops. The primary risks mirror many of the themes for ESPs: executives who are unaware of the account situation, promises that can't be kept, real-time agreements that aren't in the supplier's best interest, undermined key account manager authority, poor customer experiences and damaged relationships.

As indicated in Figure 6.3, ensuring maximum impact from the resources and energy invested in top-to-tops requires a systematic and carefully executed business process.

Top-to-tops are a two-way street and may not be appropriate for all key accounts. Account teams need to consider the mutual benefits that are possible based on each account's specific situation, opportunities and relationship status. Top-to-tops that don't result in meaningful actions aren't beneficial to either organization and, in some cases, do more damage than good.

Much of the success of top-to-tops comes down to high-quality pre-meeting planning and post-meeting follow-through. In this

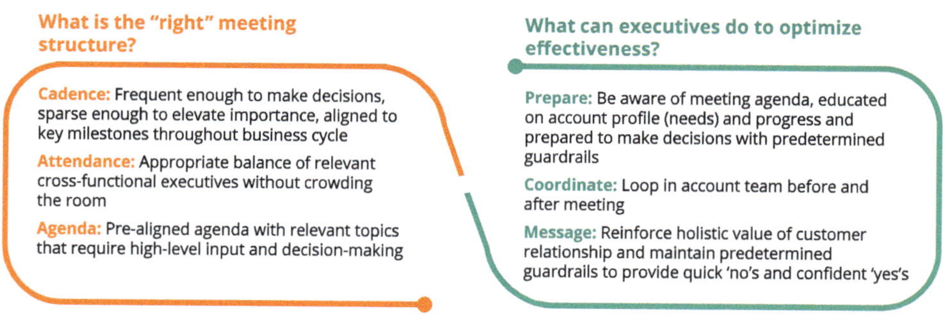

Figure 6.3 *Keys to high-impact top-to-tops.*

regard, the best organizations formulate top-to-top playbooks and processes and commit time and energy into executing these processes with rigor. While this sounds obvious, the demands on executives can make it difficult to get the time and focus necessary for success. For this reason, the priority must be on the quality of top-to-tops rather than quantity. In other words, less can be more.

CONCLUDING THOUGHTS

When it comes to KAM, customers and competitors require careful navigation, but they aren't the biggest challenge. For most organizations, that comes from within. This is especially true in life sciences. Brand-centric strategic planning, transactional one-to-one selling models and cross-functional and cross-BU silos have served the industry well—but they run counter to the organization-wide alignment and support required for KAM to succeed.

Strong senior executive alignment and engagement is critical to achieving the organization-wide clarity and cross-functional execution required to maximize success with complex and strategically critical key accounts. Indeed, it's truly a make-or-break prospect for KAM programs.

CHAPTER SEVEN

KAM Program Office: Marshalling the internal support required for results

Mike Moorman

Marshalling the cross-functional internal support required for key account management (KAM) is challenging for any organization. This is especially true in life sciences, where brand-centric marketing, physician-focused sales models and siloed business units have long been sources of success. KAM is a relatively newer and entirely different go-to-market strategy that requires new and different types of cross-functional support as compared against life sciences' traditional model. As a result, many internal functions have had difficulty pivoting to KAM and providing the resources and expertise needed to support KAM while continuing to meet the many demands of the traditional commercial model. And some functional leaders in life sciences

DOI: 10.4324/9781003226512-7

may still view KAM as a role rather than an organization-wide business strategy, which contributes to the challenges.

One approach that has helped other industries achieve critical cross-functional alignment and support for KAM is the KAM Program Office (KPO), sometimes referred to as the KAM Center of Excellence (CoE). KPOs ensure the organization is adopting leading practices, harmonizing KAM strategies and processes organizationwide and delivering the cross-functional support required for success. KPOs have helped KAM pioneers such as Siemens[1] and others achieve world-class KAM effectiveness and impact.

However, despite their effectiveness, ZS research[2] indicates that, to date, only a minority of life sciences companies have implemented an effective KPO. The adoption and advancement of KPOs therefore represent a major opportunity for many life sciences organizations.

In this chapter, we provide insights on designing an effective KPO, including mission definition and optimal structure and operating model design. But first, we dig a little deeper into the current challenges and opportunities many life sciences companies are experiencing that KPOs can help address.

RESOURCE FRAGMENTATION AND DISPARATE EFFORTS UNDERMINE KAM IMPACT

As life sciences companies have sought to build and improve their KAM strategies, many have been hampered by fragmented cross-functional support and disparate efforts from one business unit to the next. One explanation for this struggle is that KAM requires new and different types of cross-functional support relative to traditional life sciences models. Another is that cross-functional leaders must continue to support many of the traditional approaches while simultaneously building the new capabilities and support required for KAM.

The norm in life sciences has long been brand- or product-centric, one-to-one physician and surgeon selling coupled with business unit autonomy. This traditional approach has been amazingly successful and has greatly benefited patients, healthcare providers and manufacturers alike. Over the years, internal functions including marketing, human resources (HR), training, analytics, operations and legal and compliance have carefully tuned their capabilities to best support these approaches.

Conversely, KAM involves customer-centric business-to-business (B2B) strategies and capabilities that address a diverse mix of decision makers, objectives and priorities associated with large and complex provider and payer systems and groups. KAM is an organization-wide business strategy that requires very different value strategies, customer engagement processes, operating models, competencies, training, metrics, motivation systems, data and tools than traditional life sciences models.

The KAM360™ framework shown in Figure 7.1 defines the cross-functional capabilities that are most critical to KAM and provides a reference for functional leaders as they assess their organization's role in supporting KAM success.

The accelerated adoption of KAM in life sciences is forcing every internal function to rapidly assess its role in supporting and enabling the capabilities illustrated in Figure 7.1, as well as the implications for how the function then structures and resources its teams. For example:

- Marketing organizations are learning to design and enable advanced B2B offerings and value propositions that can be tailored to the needs of complex organized customer segments and individual accounts.

- HR functions are working to understand the competencies required by different types of KAM value strategies and to innovate competency models and people selection accordingly. At the same time, they're innovating motivation systems for key account managers and for improving teamwork across customer-facing roles.
- Training functions are developing the unique learning journeys KAM requires in life sciences, both for key account managers themselves as well as for other customer-facing roles and internal stakeholders who play critical parts of the KAM equation.
- Operations teams are working to understand the data and tools required for KAM, how these needs are different from those for traditional sales forces and physician-level marketing, and how they can effectively support both.
- Analytics teams are learning how best to enable KAM strategy decisions, performance management metrics and individual key account managers.
- Legal and compliance teams are navigating how best to guide commercial-medical interactions and new ways of partnering and communicating value with organized customers.

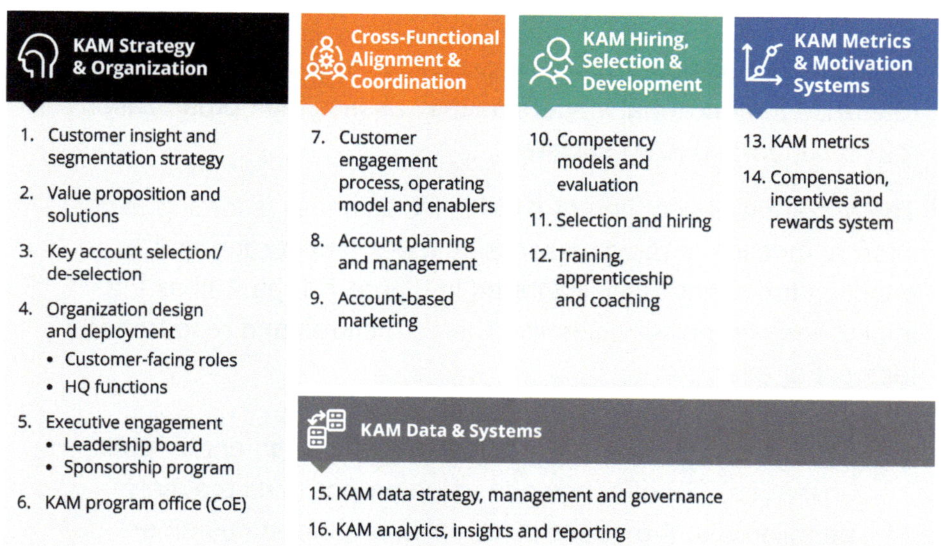

Figure 7.1 *KAM is an organization-wide business strategy (KAM360™ framework).*

Ultimately, the resources and capabilities each function brings forward must combine to provide the integrated support system required to maximize KAM impact and return on investment. Unfortunately, many life sciences organizations experience something very different. Siloed efforts across functions and business units often result in a hodgepodge of KAM support and approaches. For many supporting functions, KAM has become an add-on responsibility often relegated to a second or third priority, particularly as these same functions must continue to support brand marketing and large field sales forces. And different business units in the same company often pursue their own approaches to KAM—reinventing the wheel, failing to adopt leading KAM practices and failing to harmonize strategies and practices to maximize collective impact with the company's most important customers.

The solution is a centralized approach for defining and orchestrating effective best practices, cross-functional roles, resources and execution. Creation of a KPO that includes representation from the cross-section of commercial functions critical to KAM success is a means to this end.

KPO SCOPE AND ROLES FOLLOW MISSION

KPOs focus on four key objectives. They seek to ensure that the organization is: (1) adopting leading KAM practices; (2) connecting and harmonizing strategy, processes and tools across functions, business units and regions; (3) delivering or facilitating the ongoing cross-functional support required for KAM success; and (4) achieving continuous improvement.

KPOs often operate as a combination of fully and partially dedicated cross-functional team members through a mix of direct and matrixed reporting. While some team members will report and be fully dedicated to the KPO, others may continue to report into their various functions and be either fully or partially dedicated to KAM. The guiding principle is that the KPO brings together the right combination of individuals and roles to ensure that KAM is being prioritized and expertly supported organizationwide.

The KPO's scope of responsibility varies from one organization to the next, as does team composition, reporting relationships and operating model. The KAM360™ framework (Figure 7.1) provides a valuable reference for establishing a KPO's scope of responsibility, which can vary from "own" to "advise" or "informed" for aspects of each of the 16 KAM drivers. As an example, consider the scope of responsibilities for one leading company's KPO as depicted in Table 7.1.

Determining the optimal scope of responsibility for a KPO requires an assessment of effectiveness, efficiency, agility and accountability trade-offs. Broader organizational structure, operating models, capabilities and culture all come into play when assessing these factors—as does the KAM value strategy and KAM organizational structure itself.

Based on our experience, guiding principles for deciding a KPO's scope of responsibility include the following:

1. KPOs should play stronger roles for critical KAM effectiveness drivers that meet any of the following conditions:
    - Are otherwise likely to be under-resourced and under-prioritized
    - Have strong interdependencies with other key drivers of KAM effectiveness that span functions and need to be closely harmonized
    - Are newer to the organization and require deep expertise in KAM that may not exist within supporting functions

Table 7.1 *KAM Program Office (KPO) scope of responsibility case example*

Activity	Role	Scope
Advise KAM strategy, processes, motivation systems and tools design	Advise	• Executive communications • KAM segmentation, value strategy and organization design • KAM metrics and compensation plans design • CRM and systems requirements • New product launch planning • Commercial transformations
Manage ongoing business processes	Own	• Key account selection and deselection process • Metrics tracking and reporting • Executive sponsorship program • Ad hoc analytics • Content for KAM Executive Board
Govern harmonized processes and enablers	Own	• Customer engagement process and operating model • Account planning frameworks and tools • Advanced solutions collateral and tools • KAM competency models and role descriptions • KAM competency evaluation tools and guidelines • Incentive compensation design frameworks and guidelines • KAM training and development
Drive continuous improvement in organization-wide KAM effectiveness	Own	• External and internal leading practices benchmarking • KAM strategy and capabilities effectiveness evaluations, investment priorities and business cases • Continuous improvement initiatives
Stay abreast of broader internal issues and flag KAM interdependencies	Informed	• Broader marketing, sales, medical, analytics, HR, training and legal and compliance plans • KAM interdependencies and coordination

2. KPOs should typically "advise" rather than "own" strategic decisions that require diverse leadership agreement across functions, business units or regions. A litmus-test question for ownership versus advisement is the following:
   - "Is it appropriate for the senior-most leader responsible for the KAM function to own this decision on behalf of the entire organization?" If the answer is "no," then the KPO should likely be an advisor rather than owner.
3. KPO "ownership" can vary in scope and include one or more of the following responsibilities:
   - "Designing" the related strategy, processes or enablers (e.g., designing the KAM metrics and dashboards)
   - "Managing" a given process or enabler, including accountability for associated deliverables and impact (e.g., running ongoing performance reporting or annual key account selection and deselection)
   - "Disseminating and governing" strategy, processes or enablers, including ensuring effective adoption and execution (e.g., ensuring that all business units are adopting defined customer engagement processes or KAM competency models)
4. KPO ownership of a given driver can be accomplished either through a fully dedicated KPO team or by an extended team led by a core KPO team member. Options include:
   - Self-contained KPO ownership, in which all resources and people necessary to fulfill the role are dedicated to the KPO
   - Matrixed ownership, in which a functional leader who's a member of the KPO oversees fulfillment of the role through resources that sit within their respective functional organization

KPOs can also be tiered or distributed, with an enterprise-level KPO working in tandem with business-unit-level KPOs, for instance. In the next section, we delve deeper into KPO structure and team composition considerations.

KPO STRUCTURES AND TEAM COMPOSITION ARE NOT ONE-SIZE-FITS-ALL

A KPO's structure and operating model design follows from a clear definition of its scope of responsibilities and a consideration of the company's broader structure, resources and operating model. KPOs generally report directly or indirectly to a senior-most KAM leader while also serving the KAM Executive Board.

KPOs must deliver cost-effective KAM support while ensuring clear cross-functional accountabilities. While KPO structure varies by company, structures generally fall within one of three broad archetypes as depicted in Figure 7.2.

In the first archetype, a **centralized KPO** has enterprise-wide responsibility for supporting and enabling the KAM strategy and effectiveness. In this case, the KPO collaborates closely with different functions and business units to ensure necessary resources, expertise and execution.

In the **distributed KPO** described in the second archetype, a centralized KPO orchestrates with one or more sub-KPOs at the business-unit level to address enterprise-wide KAM needs while also delivering support that might be highly specific to KAM within a specific business. For instance, the KAM function within an oncology-focused business unit might require oncology-specific expertise to support account profiling, advanced solutions, analytics and other activities the oncology KAM function requires. In this case, the oncology business unit might maintain a sub-KPO that meets the oncology-specific needs while closely orchestrating with the enterprise KPO on enterprise-wide best practices and harmonization.

In the third archetype, which incorporates a **KAM Center of Excellence**, a large proportion of the KPO's responsibility and

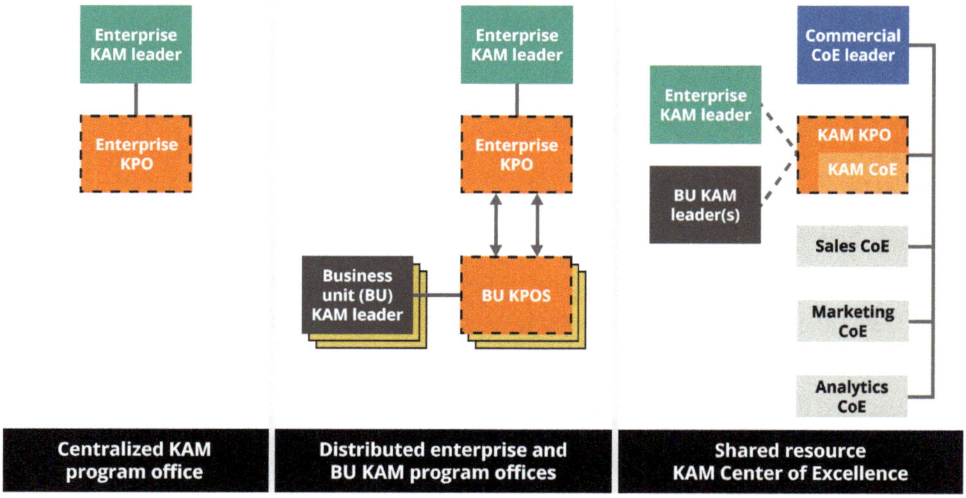

Figure 7.2 *Three KAM Program Office (KPO) structure archetypes.*

resources sits in a KAM-focused Center of Excellence (CoE). In this case, the CoE serves both KAM leadership and the KAM Executive Board as a member of the KPO (or instead of a KPO) and provides a conduit to resources within various business functions.

Team composition and KPO team size will vary according to the office's defined scope of responsibilities and its structural archetype. The guiding principle is to achieve a "light" fully dedicated team and to leverage functional resources to tap into expertise and gain efficiency. Table 7.2 provides an example of one life sciences company's KPO team composition.

KPO structure and composition must ensure the KPO brings together the right combination of individuals and roles to ensure KAM is being prioritized and expertly supported organizationwide. At the same time, the team's size and composition should be cost-effective and manageable while ensuring impact and accountability.

Table 7.2 *KAM Program Office (KPO) team composition case example*

KPO Team Member	Role	KPO Reporting
Vice President of KAM	KAM Leader; KPO Leader; KAM Executive Board Chairperson	KPO reports to VP KAM
KPO Director	KPO Team Leader; Functional Lead: • Account selection and deselection • KAM metrics and reporting • Ad hoc analytics support • Executive sponsor program • Customer engagement process; account planning processes and enablers • KAM Executive Board support	Full-time Direct reporting
KPO Analyst	KPO Functional Support	Full-time Direct reporting
Segment and Account-Based Marketing Director	Functional Lead: • Segmentation • Advanced offerings, value propositions and assets • Account-based marketing	Full-time Matrixed reporting
Director of Sales Operations	Functional Lead: • Data, systems and tools	Part-time Matrixed reporting
Director of Commercial Analytics	Functional Lead: • Supporting analytics for KAM	Part-time Matrixed reporting
Medical Director	Functional Lead: • MSL alignment	Part-time Matrixed reporting
HR Director	Functional Lead: • KAM competency models, evaluation and selection • KAM learning journey • KAM incentives compensation	Part-time Matrixed reporting
Legal and Regulatory Director	Functional Lead: • KAM-related legal and regulatory guidance and oversight	Part-time Matrixed reporting

CONCLUDING THOUGHTS

Most life sciences companies are still relatively early on their KAM journey, and many are struggling to effectively harmonize and cross-functionally support their KAM strategy and organizations. KAM requires new and different types of support relative to traditional life sciences models, which remain important even as KAM has become a priority. Organizations that employ both enterprise-level KAM teams and business-unit KAM teams face an even more complex challenge.

An effective KAM Program Office provides companies with a way to ensure the organization-wide support, expertise and harmonization necessary for maximum KAM impact and return on investment. KPOs have proven to be highly impactful in other industries and hold the same promise for life sciences.

NOTES

1 Mike Moorman and Strategic Account Management Association, "Siemens AG: organizing account management around customers."
2 ZS and Strategic Account Management Association, "State of Key Account Management in Pharma" and "State of Key Account Management in Medtech," Q4 2020.

CHAPTER EIGHT

The long and short of KAM metrics

Mike Moorman, Jude Konzelmann and Namita Powers

In the past few years, life sciences companies have increasingly embraced the practice of key account management (KAM) to strengthen and grow their customer relationships. At some point along this new KAM journey, leadership will rightly ask, "What results are we achieving?" This simple question raises complex issues about how the KAM program should be measured and what success looks like. In an ideal world, a single financial KPI would tell the tale. Unfortunately, with KAM, that's not the case.

The subject of KAM metrics is complicated in any industry, and life sciences is no exception. Here are some major reasons why:

- **Longer time horizons** required to identify, develop and deliver new solutions that move beyond the pill or beyond the product
- **High complexity** associated with business-to-business customer engagement models and associated requirements for organization-wide collaboration and orchestration

DOI: 10.4324/9781003226512-8

- **Challenging hurdles** associated with data integration and completeness for large and complex payer and provider systems, plus difficulty collecting data from account teams
- **Less familiarity** at the executive level with KAM relative to traditional life sciences models

KAM demands a robust approach to measurement and expectations-setting. At the same time, the stakes are high. Clearly agreed metrics and expectations play a critical role in KAM program performance management and in gaining and keeping senior executive alignment and support. In this chapter, we introduce five key principles that are critical to KAM program metrics for the pharmaceutical and medtech industries.

PRINCIPLE NO. 1: THINK "BALANCED SCORECARD"

The search for a single metric for KAM is, in many ways, the search for a unicorn. KAM is a multifaceted and multiyear journey. For new KAM programs, measurable financial outcomes may take one to two years to emerge. And even for mature programs, the solution development, implementation and pull-through cycles for any one key account can easily span fiscal years. KAM takes a longer-term strategic orientation to customer engagement, relationships and value co-creation than traditional life sciences models.

The long cycle times associated with KAM mean that outcomes metrics will show little for new KAM programs or recently added key accounts and will never fully illuminate progress for longer-term opportunities.

For these reasons, KAM requires a balanced scorecard comprising both leading and lagging metrics. Figure 8.1 highlights examples of potential metrics for the life sciences industry.

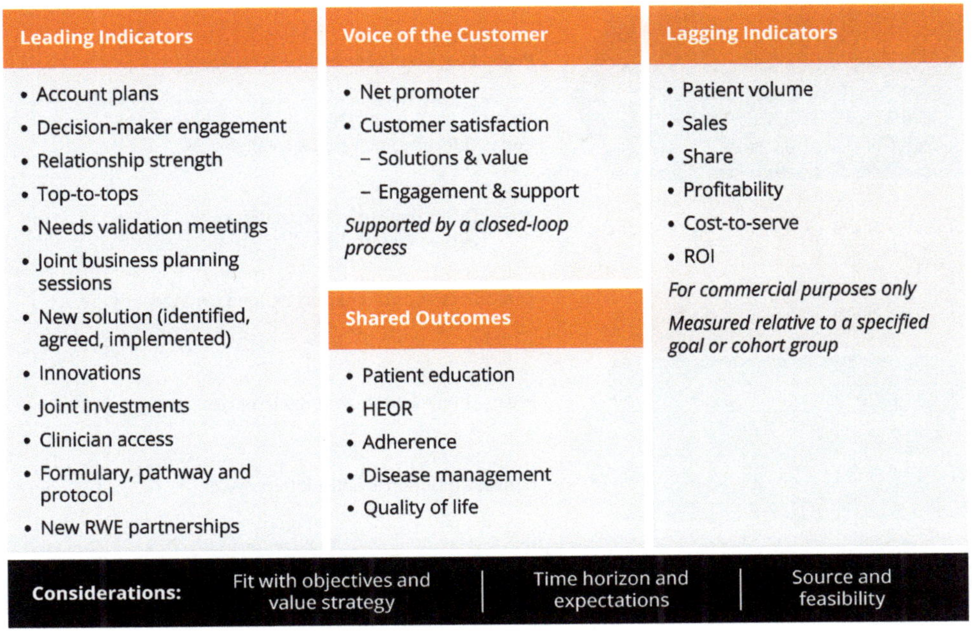

Figure 8.1 *Examples of potential KAM metrics.*

Lagging metrics measure outcomes. KAM is a business strategy, and outcomes include volume, sales, revenue, profit or ROI. Most organizations don't try to track all of these, and profit and ROI are the most difficult. Some organizations also emphasize that these types of outcomes are for "commercial purposes only." This is to underscore that there are medical or other non-commercial outcomes that are also important goals for the KAM program. Examples can include shared outcomes that both the life sciences company and the organized customer might measure together. The way in which commercial outcomes are reported and used internally and externally must conform to regulatory and compliance standards.

Causality can be a challenge to prove when it comes to lagging metrics and the outcomes that can be directly attributed to KAM. Even when outcomes can be measured for key accounts, it's not always easy to attribute the KAM program's impact on those outcomes. Figure 8.2 illustrates three key approaches for

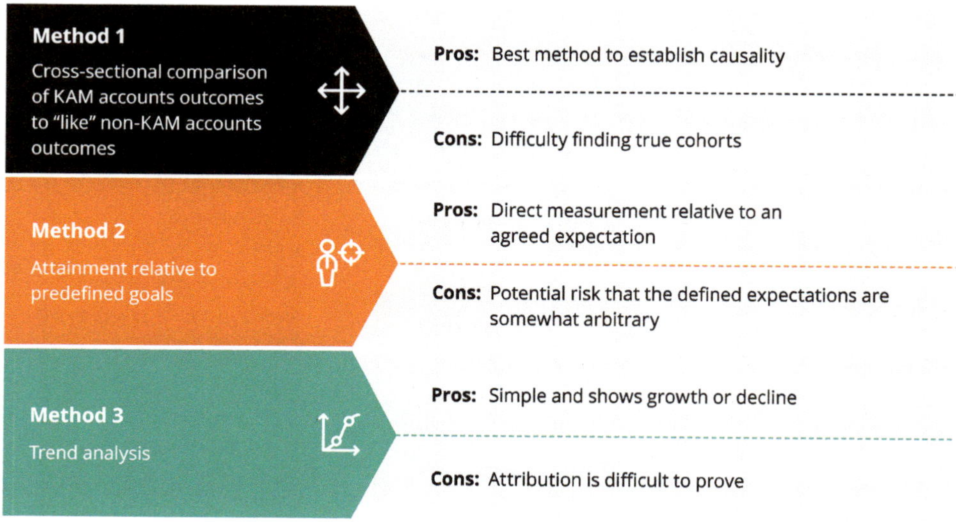

Figure 8.2 *Alternative approaches to measuring KAM's impact on outcomes.*

measuring KAM impact on outcomes and the associated pros and cons.

Because of KAM's long cycle times, lagging measures focused on outcomes will never tell the full story. Leading metrics help to close the gap by providing a more complete picture of performance along dimensions critical to outcomes. The catch is that the leading metrics must be direct and significant precursors to the outcomes sought by the program.

For instance, better **strategic account planning** might be a major priority and leading metric for the KAM program that, if achieved, will ultimately drive greater financial outcomes. Better engaging a broader and more senior group of customer decision makers might be a critical priority for the KAM program, leading to a **stakeholder engagement** or a **relationship strength** leading metric. Specific customer solutions might have observable milestones associated with commitment, implementation and pull-through, in which cases the type and number of **solution milestones** achieved could be a leading indicator.

PRINCIPLE NO. 2: LET CONTEXT DRIVE YOUR DECISIONS

New KAM programs will rely heavily on leading indicators, while more mature programs will lean toward lagging indicators. That said, both types of indicators should always be included. Even for highly advanced KAM programs, leading indicators continue to be critical levers for performance management.

Yet, the list of potential leading metrics is expansive. What defines the right leading metrics is situational based on the company's current stage in the KAM journey and associated priorities. Data availability is also a key consideration. In some cases, the data might need to be self-reported by individual key account managers, which is sufficient if a quality control mechanism is in place.

To determine which metrics are the right ones, a company needs to answer several questions:

1. **Strategic intent**: What unique types of financial, clinical and patient experience benefits is the KAM program seeking to create for each segment of key accounts, and what benefits will our company achieve as a result?
2. **Use case**: Who's going to use the metrics and what do they most need to support the decisions and actions they want to take? (For example, the CEO might have different needs than the leader of the KAM program.)
3. **Maturity**: Where are we in our program maturity and which metrics are the most critical to focus on at this stage in our journey?
4. **Viability**: What data would we need and how accessible is that data to us at this time?

The right KAM program metrics may evolve as the program evolves and as the answers to the above four questions change.

This is particularly true for the leading metrics. At the same time, leadership will want to ensure some stability in a core set of metrics so the company can track progress over time.

PRINCIPLE NO. 3: EMPHASIZE VOICE OF THE CUSTOMER

It's debatable whether voice of the customer (VOC) metrics are leading or lagging indicators. In some ways, VOC metrics are between the two ends of the spectrum. What's not debatable are the powerful insights and impact VOC KAM metrics generate.

VOC KAM metrics seek to measure at least the following: the degree to which key accounts have a positive and superior experience as a result of the KAM program; how much new value key accounts are realizing relative to their key priorities as a result of the KAM program; and any relationship risks or unaddressed needs that have cropped up.

VOC metrics that prove advancement in customer experience and value perception are highly compelling for leadership and KAM program stakeholders companywide. In addition, when captured at the account and decision influencer level, these metrics greatly improve individual account planning, follow-up and broader performance management.

The real-time understanding of relationship risks and unaddressed needs that VOC provides can be a game-changer. The very best KAM VOC approaches are "closed-loop" in nature. Any identified risks or unaddressed needs are conveyed in real time to the right individuals in the KAM organization, who then take immediate action. Rapid and effective response can save or greatly improve relationships which, in the case of KAM, has huge financial implications.

VOC metrics are nearly as powerful as financial outcomes in proving KAM impact. Organizations that don't institute a robust VOC approach for key accounts are missing a major opportunity.

In addition to VOC, the value of success stories from the field also warrants attention. Lagging outcomes metrics don't tell a motivating story early in a KAM program's life cycle. Engaging senior leadership during these early stages can be quite challenging, even with great leading metrics. Individual and textured case examples that bring this impact to life can go a long way. The key is to have a systematic way of capturing and communicating these bright spots up the chain.

PRINCIPLE NO. 4: DON'T GET DERAILED BY DILUTION

The number of accounts in life sciences KAM programs varies significantly from one company to the next. For KAM programs focused on IDNs, IPPNs and large group practices, it's not uncommon to have 80–150 accounts in the program. With this number of accounts, some subsegments of accounts invariably are more ready and better candidates for KAM than others. And not all accounts will be equally receptive to the types of solutions the KAM program offers at a given point in time.

Thus, metrics that are simply averaged across all key accounts risk showing diluted impact, especially in KAM's first few years. The faster-moving subsegments will get "averaged down" by the slower-moving subsegments. This makes it hard to understand the size of impact and where the KAM program is driving its greatest results versus lesser results. Senior leaders looking at averaged results might prematurely conclude the KAM program isn't having enough impact and fail to see the more significant impact in higher-readiness subsegments. Furthermore, KAM is not a one-size-fits-all program. Different types of KAM models often are deployed for different key account segments.

The answer is to define meaningful subgroups and then measure at the subgroup level. Subgroup dimensions might include total addressable market, control, risk assumption, willingness to partner, type of institution and other possible dimensions. A particularly advanced practice is to include a “local healthcare market” archetype as one of the subgroup metrics. Ultimately, the point is to pick dimensions that are most correlated with the KAM program strategy and priorities and factors that most affect expected size and speed of impact.

PRINCIPLE NO. 5: SOLIDIFY LEADERSHIP ALIGNMENT

We started this chapter by asking the leadership question, “What results are we achieving?” Up to this point, we have provided insights related to designing metrics that will best answer this question.

The last point we want to make is equally as important. The process of designing KAM program metrics is itself one of the best opportunities to strengthen senior leadership understanding, alignment and support for the KAM program more broadly—the lack of which is one of the top reasons KAM programs fail.

Consider a common situation: Many members of the senior leadership team may have risen through the ranks in the traditional life sciences model. Yet, success in the traditional life sciences model has been based on more transactional reach-frequency approaches, promotional detailing approaches and brand or product centricity. KAM is nearly the opposite of these models. As a result, many leaders may not fully understand KAM, what it is or what it takes—through no fault of their own.

At least three major interactions should occur with senior leadership when designing KAM metrics:

1. One-on-one conversations to solicit input on KAM program objectives and priorities
2. Meeting(s) to assess alternative metrics relative to context
3. Meeting(s) to finalize metrics and associated expectations

Each represents a valuable opportunity to improve senior executives' understanding of KAM and to build alignment on what success looks like. For example, if senior executives believe a new KAM program will show significant financial impact in one month, they're likely to be disappointed. KAM program leaders need to manage such unrealistic expectations early.

These interactions also provide an opportunity to identify important gaps in the KAM program. For example, a lack of clear KAM program objectives and value strategy frequently comes to light during metrics discussions. When objectives and value strategy are unclear, it's impossible to confidently specify the right metrics. In this case, the organization needs to take a step back and clarify its KAM objectives and strategy before proceeding.

KAM program metrics design provides exactly the right opportunity to inform and align the executive team. If done right, the result is not only the right metrics, but also the right support critical for success.

CONCLUDING THOUGHTS

While determining the right KAM program metrics is complex, getting it right is critical for managing and improving the program and generating and maintaining executive support. The five principles introduced here are designed to help manage that complexity, so KAM programs are measured on the appropriate mix of leading, VOC and lagging indicators based on the program's objectives, value strategy and maturity.

CHAPTER NINE

Customer engagement process: The secret to agile execution

Mike Moorman and Namita Powers

Most pharmaceutical and medtech companies have taken meaningful steps in their key account management (KAM) journey. In many cases, they've selected key accounts and put in place a KAM organization, creating a strong foundation. Thus, it would seem logical that what remains is to sort out metrics and incentives, conduct training and declare victory. In fact, many companies have followed exactly that path—only to be disappointed. A critical ingredient is missing.

KAM is an organization-wide business strategy and, in life sciences, requires a new approach for engaging complex organized customers—one that shifts from the industry's traditional "inside out" approach to a more customer-centric "outside in" perspective. It's a team sport, requiring new and significant organization-wide coordination and collaboration. In fact, one of the biggest barriers to KAM cited time and again has nothing to do with customers or

DOI: 10.4324/9781003226512-9

competitors. It's internal silos. Experienced practitioners will tell you the real KAM challenge often comes from within.

The backbone of KAM success, and in some ways the secret sauce, is a well-defined and operationalized customer engagement process (CEP) and associated operating model. In this chapter, we define the critical attributes for an effective and agile CEP and provide implementation and change management insights based on extensive experience in life sciences and a dozen other business-to-business (B2B) industries.

CASE EXAMPLE: A FAMILIAR PATTERN

To appreciate the critical role of CEP, consider one leading pharmaceutical company's situation. The company had completed a rigorous assessment of organized customer needs, decision processes, control, risk assumption and partnering orientation. Based on the insights generated, the company then segmented and selected accounts and implemented a new organization design. The strategy was comprehensive and addressed the basic roles, number and deployment of the portfolio KAMs, business unit KAMs and many other commercial and medical customer-facing roles. Training and account plans development followed. The organization thought it had clarity and alignment. So why was leadership surprised by the lack of change and impact that followed? A post-launch audit revealed the following:

- Key account managers succeeded at basic contracting but struggled to elevate themselves to strategic relationships and programs, even though they had been trained in B2B strategic selling.
- Role confusion and conflict plagued internal coordination between customer-facing roles. The problem was especially pronounced between the enterprise key

account managers and the business unit key account managers; the business unit key account managers and the hospital sales representatives; and the commercial team and the medical team.

- Internal functions were unsure how best to support the KAM teams and lacked the resources and focus necessary to do so.
- KAM teams presented clearly beneficial solutions and programs to customers, but, in many cases, couldn't motivate the customers enough to act.
- In other cases, customers got excited about new solutions and programs, but the company was unable to execute because of its own internal issues. Customers were left disappointed.

THE CRITICAL ROLE OF AGILE CEP

CEP's importance in complex selling and delivery environments was recognized as far back as the 1980s. IBM's Signature Selling Method (SSM) is an example. SSM defined IBM's approach for engaging and coordinating organizationwide to tailor and deliver superior B2B value. A well-designed and operationalized CEP was central to IBM's evolution from a transactional product organization to a solutions provider.

CEPs define and structure the critical engagement "phases" at each stage of the customer journey. The best CEPs comprehensively illuminate the underlying details for each phase. As shown in Figure 9.1, these include phase-specific objectives, advances, activities, roles and enablers.

CEPs tackle two of the most challenging aspects of KAM at once: (1) moving from a transactional engagement approach to one that is customer-centric and focused on mutually valuable solutions;

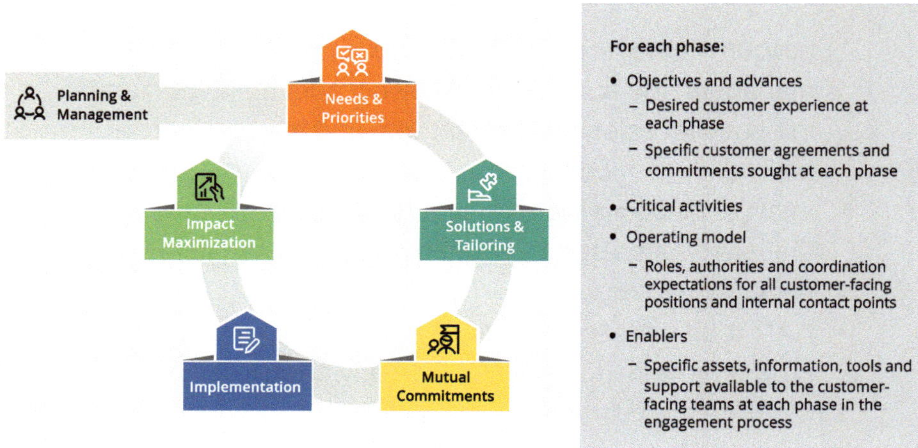

Figure 9.1 *An example Customer Engagement Process (CEP).*
Note: This illustration shows basic phases of a CEP. The final design of phases and underlying components can vary significantly by company.

and (2) coordinating and collaborating between customer-facing roles and internal roles to effectively align and execute at each phase of the CEP.

In life sciences, reach frequency and centrally prescribed messaging has been an extraordinarily effective one-to-one HCP engagement model for decades. KAM and CEP are nearly the opposite of this deeply entrenched model. Key accounts are a more complex network of diverse decision makers and influencers, each with their own needs and priorities. Key accounts may have multiple departments and locations, each responding to a dynamic and rapidly evolving healthcare environment. At the same time, key account managers must orchestrate a diverse mix of their own company's commercial and medical roles, each engaging different and sometimes overlapping decision influencers at the customer.

The CEP is the backbone for elevating from transactional engagement to solutions and to the organization-wide coordination required to maximize customer experience. But not all CEPs are equal or effective. Three aspects of CEP design and implementation are especially critical to CEP success.

DON'T CONFUSE AMBIGUITY AND AGILITY

Agility is a key attribute of leading-practice CEPs. Unfortunately, many organizations confuse ambiguity for agility. The ambiguity trap is easy to spot. The CEP and operating model haven't been formally defined—or have been only at a very high level. The implicit expectation is that key account managers will individually "figure it out" with their account teams and with internal support functions. This leads to a multitude of individual CEPs and operating models, some good and many not so good. While a few rare and exceptional key account managers and associated account team members find a way to succeed, most struggle. This often leads to reverting to old habits rather than adopting the approaches that are intuitive to the very best. Ambiguity allows for latitude, but it doesn't promote effective agility.

Agility is born out of deep customer intimacy, systematic assessment of options and actions at each stage of the customer journey, and a shared "true north" organizationwide. Three especially important areas of KAM agility are the following:

- Agility to identify and tailor win-win, mutually valuable solutions specific to individual accounts' unique needs and priorities
- Agility to effectively and efficiently coordinate customer-facing roles and internal support at every stage of the customer journey as required to successfully implement different solutions and programs
- Agility to track impact relative to expectations at the account level and to identify gaps and real-time actions to maximize mutual value

By establishing a dynamic and repeatable organization-wide approach for each stage of customer engagement, CEPs can turn agility into an organizational core competency. This point is so important that it's worth repeating: An effective CEP is central to effective agility.

DESIGN FOR THE RIGHT LEVEL OF DETAIL

Effective CEPs are customized and fit for purpose. Customer decision journeys, value strategies, go-to-market models and regulatory requirements are unique in life sciences. They also vary by company, based on portfolio and organization structure. Generic and off-the-shelf CEPs fail to address these critical differences. They lead to watered-down execution or worse. At the same time, over-engineered CEPs end up on a shelf. The art in designing CEPs is to achieve the level of detail that provides organization-wide focus and clarity while simultaneously remaining user-friendly. It's not an easy balance to strike.

We've found that five key approaches stand out when designing agile CEPs:

1. **Start with the customer:** Anchor the CEP in a deep understanding of the customer journey. CEPs should be end to end, spanning from needs identification all the way through implementation and value maximization.
2. **Co-create as a team:** Start with CEP leading practices and engage a cross-functional team to customize the CEP. Address activities, interactions and expectations for customer-facing roles as well as internal roles. Use the design process to identify and address the more sensitive and contentious aspects of roles, authorities and accountabilities. Don't let these land mines go unaddressed.
3. **Define a shared "true north":** Be specific about the customer experience objectives, customer agreements and internal agreements that constitute the "objectives" and

"advances" at each CEP phase. These provide the North Star that helps the team operate with shared purpose. They are the critical waypoints for building customer commitment and ultimately achieving mutual value.

4. **Dig deeper on likely tension points:** Get the right balance between level of detail and simplicity. CEPs that try to address all possible situations often die under their own weight. Use techniques like ZS Spotlights™ and ZS Event Specific Plays (ESPs™) to provide more granularity for the select circumstances where more specificity significantly increases KAM team effectiveness.
5. **Prioritize critical enablers:** Conduct a detailed assessment of existing assets and enablers available to the key account teams at each CEP stage. Objectively evaluate gaps and establish priorities that help internal functions focus their support efforts and resources.

SPEND MOST OF YOUR EFFORT ON IMPLEMENTATION AND CHANGE

It may be tempting to think that once you've designed an agile CEP that conveys the "what and how" people need to engage, you're primed for success. However, the real challenge then begins: changing deeply entrenched beliefs, behaviors and skills across the organization. "Living" the KAM CEP is easily the most difficult aspect of KAM.

Let's start with what doesn't work. Here's a conventional and common approach to CEP implementation:

- A headquarters team designs a well-thought-out CEP
- Leadership strongly communicates the CEP's implementation is critical and they expect everyone to adopt the new approaches
- HR rolls out a terrific CEP training program that's well-received by those attending

It shouldn't be a surprise if this sequence sounds familiar. In one of our courses at Northwestern University's Kellogg Executives Program, we ask for a show of hands from leaders who have experienced this approach. Course after course, nearly every hand in the room goes up. We also ask how many succeeded with this approach. Very few, and often no, hands go up. The lesson: Top-down training-based approaches to CEP and operating model change in complex selling environments simply don't work.

"Pilots" and "test and learn" approaches do better but are also prone to failure. They often lack the discipline and support required to succeed in the KAM environment. "Trial balloons" are the worst in this regard. When the paradigm is "let's see if this works" as a precursor to significant organizational commitment and support, failure is likely. With KAM and CEP, there's no sticking a toe in the water.

One method ZS has employed to address the unusual level of rigor and cross-functional commitment and enablement required for successful KAM CEP implementations is ZS Early Experience Teams (EETs™). EETs bring together design, implementation and change management into an integrated program explicitly engineered to overcome the specific change barriers associated with CEPs.

As shown in Figure 9.2, EETs are not typical "pilots" or "test and learns." They are hyper-resourced and committed first steps toward broader implementation. KAM is a must-win battle. The goal isn't to see "if" it works, but rather to learn how to "make it work." And EETs aren't just focused on the key account managers. They're focused on all the customer-facing and internal roles that must learn what it takes to effectively engage B2B customers or to execute increasingly advanced value strategies. EETs give internal roles, such as customer marketing and training, a unique opportunity to walk in the key account manager's shoes. This experience dramatically improves their understanding of the key account team's world and how they can help them succeed.

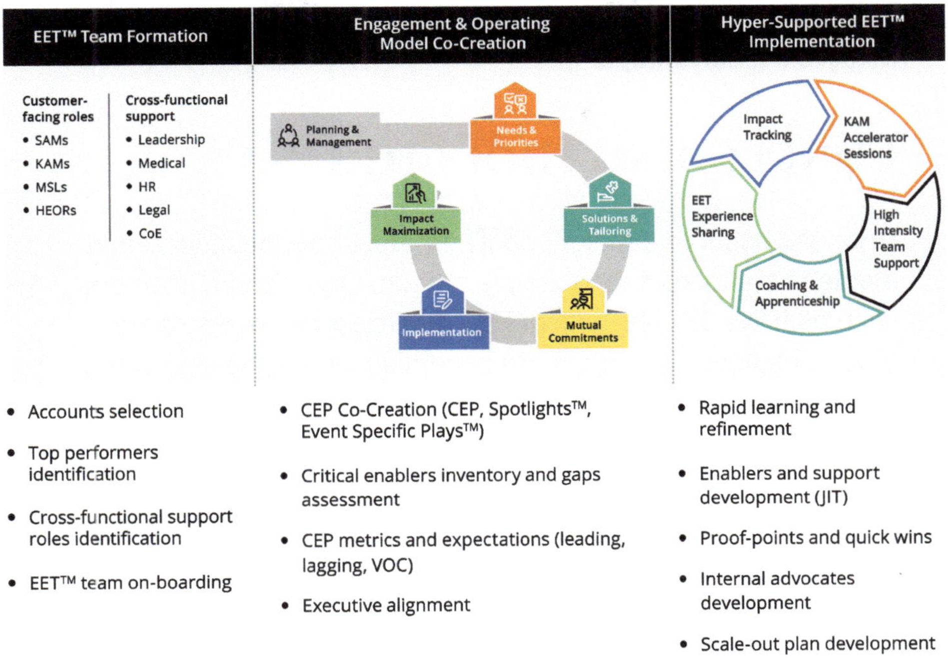

Figure 9.2 *Case example: Early experience team (EET™).*

In our experience, EETs significantly increase success rate and speed to impact by delivering the following, which are critical to change management:

- Coaching, apprenticeship and support that helps account teams rapidly apply, refine and validate the CEP
- Accelerated "wins" with key customers necessary to prove impact and generate organization-wide enthusiasm
- Clear champions and advocates who can provide testimonials about the new way of working
- Cross-functional insight on how best to support and scale KAMs based on real "hands-on" experience

Ultimately, execution excellence is what most differentiates each life sciences company's KAM program from that of its competitors. Breakthrough approaches to implementation and change management, such as EETs, are a proven and necessary way to achieve this advantage.

CONCLUDING THOUGHTS

KAM has become a major priority for most pharmaceutical and medtech companies for a simple reason: Organized customers such as IDNs, IPPNs, national payers, regional payers, large group practices and others are becoming increasingly powerful and complex. The impact of COVID-19 has elevated the importance of KAM in life sciences even further. Reduced physician access, increased formulary scrutiny, greater emphasis on risk-sharing, changing approaches to patient treatment and many other aspects of the “new normal” demand KAM-led solutions and coordination.

Most life sciences companies have taken important steps toward KAM, particularly in account selection and organization design. However, few have cracked the code on execution. Deeply entrenched reach frequency and standardized messaging, brand-centricity, commercial-medical divides and functional silos remain significant barriers to KAM in life sciences.

But it can’t continue that way. Life sciences companies must prioritize CEP design and organization-wide adoption. CEP and the associated operating model are the backbone for any KAM program and are critical to customer-centric organization-wide coordination and engagement. “Living” these new models will require innovative and purposefully engineered change management approaches specific to the challenge at hand. The ultimate goal is core competency that consistently delivers significant mutual value and sustained strategic advantage.

CHAPTER TEN

Bringing value to account planning and management

Namita Powers, Mike Powers and Alex Simon

Most life sciences companies have adopted key account models in response to the increasing consolidation and corporatization of healthcare, yet many still struggle to generate the desired impact. As one pharmacy director told us during a survey of provider organizations, "Pharma just wants to sell…their data always presents products as cost-effective, but it rarely works out that way in practice." Another said, "[Partnerships with pharma] are honestly so much work…. My staff can't handle it." Clearly, life sciences companies haven't cracked the code yet.

Pharmaceutical and medtech companies have struggled to develop customer partnerships in two major ways. First, they've generally struggled to identify partnership opportunities that are meaningful to their customers (even though many exist). Second, even when these opportunities have been identified, companies struggle to efficiently implement these partnerships

DOI: 10.4324/9781003226512-10

primarily due to cross-functional silos. For example, during a 2021 ZS roundtable, 17 industry leaders (representing about 10 life sciences organizations) discussed their KAM teams. All mentioned cross-functional collaboration as one of their biggest challenges.

The industry has rightfully turned to enhancing account planning and management capabilities as a way to combat these challenges but has typically missed the mark by oversimplifying or having too narrow a focus. Best-in-class account planning and management is not developed by creating the "best" planning templates or some "magic" technology. Instead, best-in-class account planning and management comes from a combination of rich customer insight generation, deep strategic thinking, cross-functional collaboration, disciplined preparation and execution, and KAM-focused technology that enables this holistic process.

In this chapter, we discuss the five foundational pillars that can help life sciences companies use account planning and management to unlock value across the organization.

WHAT'S THE PROBLEM WITH ACCOUNT PLANNING AND MANAGEMENT IN LIFE SCIENCES TODAY?

Pharmaceutical and medtech companies struggle with account planning and management across the board by not enabling their people, failing to create robust processes and reusing the same old technologies instead of KAM-focused account planning platforms and tools:

- **People:** Failure to enable people generally occurs when account planning is an individual rather than team effort. Moreover, one of the easiest ways to identify that a life sciences company hasn't unlocked the power of planning is when the people creating the plan view the act as an administrative burden. Once this attitude sets in, the likelihood of deep, strategic thinking is significantly reduced.

- **Processes:** Lack of robust processes largely occurs because of the typical life science company's rigidity. Unfortunately, customers typically don't make decisions in 12-month time frames that align perfectly to a life science company's planning and budgeting cycles. This inflexibility creates unrealistic expectations for account plans because the plan needs to continually adapt based on the customer's response and evolving needs. Additionally, most life science companies mistakenly believe account planning and management is a "sales exercise" and don't fully engage the marketing organization in the process. Marketing has a bird's-eye view of the overall market landscape and can gather specific customer insights in many different ways. Thus, marketing can play a critical role in enabling the KAM team to identify the customer needs that matter most, as well as the potential solutions to customer challenges the account team can pursue to drive mutual value creation.
- **Tools:** Account planning and management often sits within the sales forces' existing platforms, which have been retrofitted to support KAM. The problem is, the tools in these platforms are focused on supporting one-to-one HCP promotional selling, not coordinated team planning and integration of sales and marketing to identify solutions to customer problems. Retrofitting these legacy systems generally creates a suboptimal user experience and makes the type of collaboration needed for best-in-class account planning and management impossible.

Given these ongoing struggles, we believe five foundational pillars can help life science companies create better planning and unlock true value from account plans: collaboration process; account plan framework; technology; coaching, apprenticeship and culture; and facilitation tools and enablers (Figure 10.1).

Figure 10.1 *The five pillars of account planning and management.*

COLLABORATION PROCESS: ACCOUNT PLANNING AND MANAGEMENT IS A TEAM SPORT

Best-in-class account plans can't be created in a silo, and ensuring the right process is in place to enable collaboration is critical to success. However, life science companies have too often relied on trying to script rigidly structured meetings at a set cadence. Instead, the account planning process must be rooted in the overarching customer engagement process (CEP). When operating effectively, the account planning and management process becomes one of the most critical enablers of the CEP (Figure 10.2). Integration between the customer engagement and account planning and management processes also ensures account teams focus their planning energy on the most relevant issues at a particular time by having specific

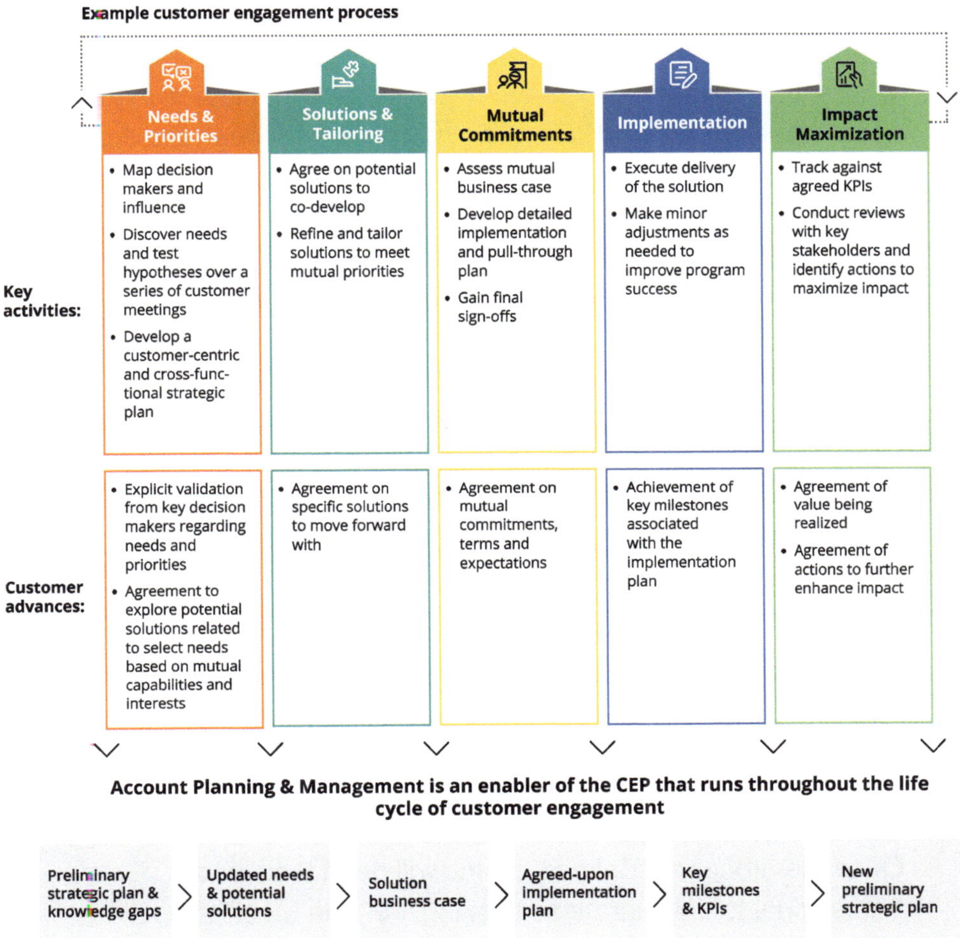

Figure 10.2 *Relationship between customer engagement process and account planning and management.*

customer advances in the engagement process trigger updates to specific sections of the account plan.

Teamwide coordination and high return on invested effort are especially important benefits of approaching account planning and management as a dynamic process linked to stages of the CEP. For example, in the initial stages of the account planning process, teams will need to hypothesize customer needs and priorities, but are often left to identify these needs by themselves. Instead, by having a clearly defined and linked process, a company can better integrate marketing into the account planning process by defining where and how marketing should support account teams in the initial stages of the CEP. Breaking down silos between the account team and marketing can help account teams better identify unique needs (by linking all of the market research in which the company is already investing to what the account teams already know about the account) while also providing more customer feedback to marketing to create improved solutions to bring to accounts. This linkage also provides clear value to all stakeholders involved in the planning and account management process so, by aligning the account planning process with the CEP, the "administrative burden" critique disappears. Instead, teams are only completing elements of the plan when they are needed, and the plan and planning process become immediately valuable and usable to their efforts.

FRAMEWORK: ENABLE STRATEGIC THINKING, NOT TEMPLATE-FILLING

Once the process is defined, teams will need tools and frameworks to drive strategic thinking. Yet, the "best" template is often mistakenly confused with a silver bullet in account planning. Several best practices can help alleviate many of the challenges with account planning today:

- Frameworks that enable strategic thinking, as opposed to account profiling, need to be the focus of the account planning template or tool. The account plan isn't meant to be a repository of everything we know about the account. Instead, the profiling information should be used as an input to support how the team arrives at a strategy. When entering an extensive amount of profiling information is a required element of the plan, teams immediately gravitate back to the "administrative burden" of needing to populate every single detail about an account, much of which can come from secondary sources.

- Multiple approaches are needed to ensure the right rigor and outputs to inform the strategic direction. To date, most templates have required a single "customer discovery" framework (often a SWOT analysis) that results in under-specified customer needs and insights generation and, ultimately, underwhelming solutions to customer challenges. By providing a wider toolkit to help KAM teams dive deeply into their customers' issues (and even the issues of the customer's customers), the resulting strategies can more effectively and specifically address customers' problems and pain points.
- When new templates are unveiled, they're often sent to the teams as a blank slate. However, account planning is a new skill for many and having clear examples of "what good looks like" and "what average looks like" will provide teams a tangible reference for what they're trying to create and show some differentiation from what they may be inclined to create.
- For the life sciences industry, headquarters needs to provide specific direction to the account teams on where and how medical and commercial can collaborate in the account planning process. Closer (compliant) collaboration between commercial and medical can unlock new opportunities and uncover unique needs within the account by capturing a holistic view of the engagement the life science company has with a particular account and all relevant stakeholders. This, in turn, allows the company to identify better solutions and better opportunities to positively impact the account and the account's patients.

TECHNOLOGY PLATFORM: USE TECHNOLOGY AS A SILO-BUSTER

With the process and the plan framework defined, the next opportunity is to enable both with a technology solution tailored for account planning and management. The right technology platform becomes the critical driver of collaboration across the account team and beyond. Today's best-in-class KAM planning platforms allow for more extensive brainstorming and collaboration across the organization, above and beyond just the field sales team. These platforms can include all functions and enable a broader set of KAM capabilities. For example, by helping engage marketing in the account planning process, these platforms begin to foster account-based marketing that allows the key account managers to tailor potential solutions identified by marketing to the unique needs of their account customers. This ability to use technology to synchronize account plans with the CEP and account-based marketing creates a powerful accelerator for the field teams' efforts. Additionally, best-in-class account planning platforms often include several forward-thinking capabilities that life science companies can take advantage of as they continue to build and advance their overall KAM capabilities:

- **Customer value-creation playbooks** help teams discover their customers' needs, align those needs with mutual opportunities and guide teams on how to tailor and implement the solution(s).
- **Value proposition repositories** allow marketing to articulate the customer benefits that can be achieved via the products, services and solutions account teams can pursue with their customers.
- **Customer impact quantification tools** compliantly estimate the business impact the life sciences company can have on its customers.
- **Cross-functional engagement collaboration capabilities** remove silos by ensuring teams constantly update each other on plan execution progress and work together to adapt the plan as they learn more through their customer engagements.
- **Seamless integration capabilities** across the CRM, reporting and analytics and marketing automation platform ecosystem help to enable KAM at scale.

For life sciences companies, the right KAM planning platform can also help overcome compliance concerns by enabling the right permissions and user access to various plan components. Moreover, the platform democratizes access to data and consolidates everything known about the account in one place—even across medical and commercial, when appropriate.

We discuss the technology needed for KAM success in more detail in Chapter 14.

COACHING, APPRENTICESHIP AND CULTURE: SET ASIDE TIME FOR DELIBERATE PRACTICE

The ability to drive deep strategic thinking will depend on a company's ability to overcome the current planning culture. Today, when executives review account plans with the team, these reviews often devolve into executives testing the account team's knowledge. Instead, once they embrace the "never complete" aspect of the plan and engage in the plan as an enabler of the CEP, executives can shift the culture by providing a sounding board to the account team based on where they are with a particular customer at any given time. If the team is still brainstorming potential needs, executives can help the team brainstorm. If the team is planning to implement a program, the executives can help identify potential blind spots the team may have missed. Once the executives set this culture of continuous learning, it can be filtered down into how the teams are trained and coached.

Since account planning and management is a team sport, these new coaching and training sessions should be done in cross-functional workshop settings to encourage practice and strategic thinking. The same is true of coaching. To develop the most impactful account plans, coaching must be available to the entire account team, not just the account manager. Making time for this apprenticeship and deliberate practice, across the entire account team, can be a truly impactful KAM success driver.

FACILITATION TOOLS AND ENABLERS: SHRINK THE BURDEN

The final pillar in building best-in-class account planning and management capabilities are the tools and enablers that facilitate the account team's processes. These go above and beyond the technology they implement and further foster the required culture change. Key enablers include:

- A running list of open questions that allows the account team to embrace the idea that they can't know everything about the account at all times, but need to remain inquisitive to try to uncover the answers.
- A business case development process and framework that helps the team build alignment and commitment for a solution, when needed, based on where the team is in the CEP.
- Progress snapshots that take many life sciences innovations in brand planning and apply them to account planning, such as building a narrative flow to the account plan and making the account team the story's protagonists.

CONCLUDING THOUGHTS

The benefits of a better planning process cut across the organization. Account teams can build a plan that actually provides value and is a tool that's constantly referenced. Marketing can use better account plans to gain insights and to create and enable better and more strategic value propositions for the company's most important customers. Executives can use a better process to drive bigger impact on the overall KAM program, both by providing better and more strategic insight into the plan and by acting as a mentor to the account manager and the broader team. And, of course, a better planning and management process will unlock more positive customer feedback, faster growth with the account and a better "win" rate.

In the end, the beneficiaries of a better account planning and management process are life sciences companies' customers. If the account plan truly becomes an enabler of the CEP, customers will have more opportunities to give specific input to the account team, helping the account team identify more important needs and build more compelling value propositions. Ultimately, that's a win for everyone involved.

CHAPTER ELEVEN

Context is king: Laying the foundation for a comprehensive KAM talent strategy

Tania Lennon, Namita Powers and Bernadette Maher

As life sciences customers continue to become increasingly organized and consolidated, it's clear life sciences companies that succeed at key account management (KAM) will have a competitive edge with customers. It's also clear that one of the most critical aspects of KAM success is getting the right talent for the role—but that's not an easy task. Defining the right talent profile and identifying the right individuals is more important than ever—especially given the focus KAM is now receiving and the significant difference between the key account manager role and life science's traditional sales rep role. Having a comprehensive KAM talent strategy, rooted in the context of the company's specific KAM strategy, model and customer engagement process, will be a key enabler of success.

DOI: 10.4324/9781003226512-11

In this chapter, we discuss talent requirements, competency model design and the ways in which competency models can drive the greatest value for the organization.

CONTEXT MATTERS: KAM ISN'T A ONE-SIZE-FITS-ALL APPROACH

The context of the key account manager role really matters, as it's not a one-size-fits-all approach. As discussed in Chapter 5, four types of account management models are common in the life sciences industry. The first of these is basic account selling (which we don't consider to be KAM), with the other three being various forms of KAM associated with increasingly sophisticated value strategies (Figure 11.1).

Most life sciences companies currently operate in the range of Type 2 to Type 3 KAM models and aspire to move to Type 3 or Type 4 KAM models over time. No single model is inherently better or worse than the others and all four have a time and a place. The right model is situational and a function of the organization's strategy, objectives and expected business impact. For instance, Type 3 KAM is the

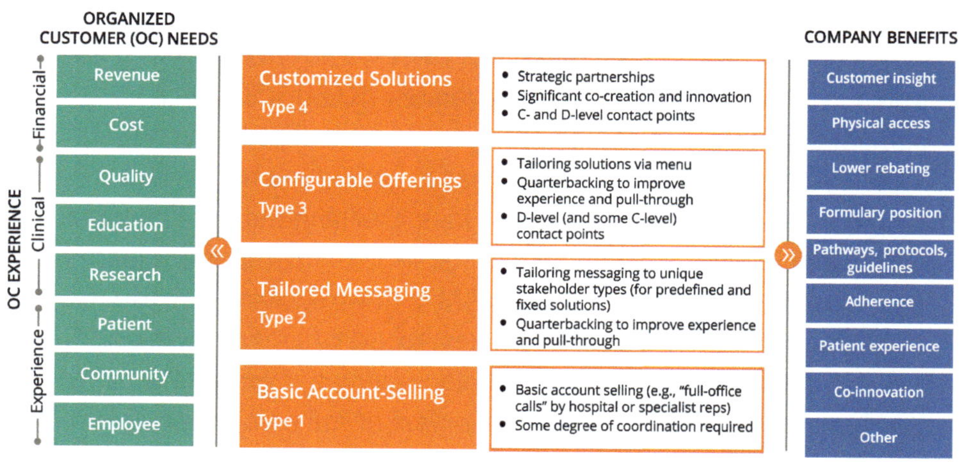

Figure 11.1 *Fundamental account management and key account management models.*

right choice if a company's strategy is focused on cost-effective scalability and tight control on solution types and positioning, while Type 4 KAM is better if the goal is one-off bespoke solutions for unique customers willing to invest in such solutions. Importantly, the value strategy and customer engagement process are different for each of the four models, which substantially impacts key account manager competency requirements.

COMPETENCY MODEL: A TOOL TO NAVIGATE THE COMPLEXITIES OF KAM TALENT

When it comes to talent, a competency model is an effective way to capture, articulate and reinforce the differences in key account manager activities and skills required by different KAM models. The best competency models go one layer beyond observable behaviors or activities, encompassing the thought process or "why" behind an action in addition to the action itself. Additionally, successful competency models delve deeper into individual characteristics, capacities and motivation (Figure 11.2).

Competency models provide a common view of performance, criteria for assessment and a roadmap for development. They

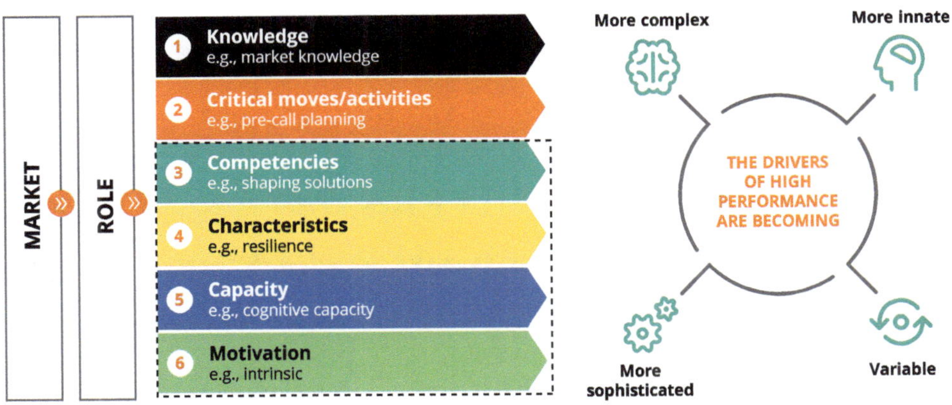

Figure 11.2 *Elements of effective competency models.*

help identify the best people for a role, given current and future measures of success; as well as behaviors indicative of success that are trainable, to shift the performance curve for the future. When developed based on objective data, competency models can be used to raise the performance bar. For example, companies focusing on proven and customized success drivers have experienced a 45% to 120% improvement in performance for sales roles, according to the *Journal of Applied Psychology.*[1] An effective competency model is a force multiplier that directly reinforces the desired value strategy and customer engagement process; enables optimal talent identification and attraction; guides coaching and training design; and influences compensation plans and motivation systems.

When developing a competency model as part of a KAM talent strategy, companies should ensure the model:

- Is grounded in the context of the KAM model, value strategy and customer engagement process (real and relevant role situations)
- Focuses on proven drivers of high performance
- Differentiates what you can develop or change in people versus what you should hire for (for instance, it recognizes the difference between competencies, characteristics, capacities and motivation)
- Emphasizes success drivers with a long-term, future orientation

WHAT ARE THE DRIVERS OF OUTSTANDING KAM PERFORMANCE?

As mentioned earlier, different KAM strategies and models require different competencies from the key account managers supporting them. But what actually drives high performance in each model? ZS research helps answer this critical question. We conducted Behavioral Event Interviews (BEIs) with 450 key account managers at 20 organizations across industries (more than half of which were in life sciences) to help us explore and confirm the success drivers in different types of key account manager roles. BEIs follow a rigorous in-depth interview process to get beneath reported data (what people say they do) to understand what truly drives performance.

Through our research, we've identified a core set of characteristics that are needed in Type 1–2 models and Type 3–4 models throughout the phases of a typical customer engagement process. Note that Type 2 key account manager competencies were more closely matched to Type 1 than they were to the more advanced Type 3. There are strong differences in what drives success within these characteristics across KAM types, and the motivational profile also differs (Figure 11.3).

In Type 1 (basic account selling) and Type 2 (entry-level KAM), the focus is on account selling, tailoring messaging and

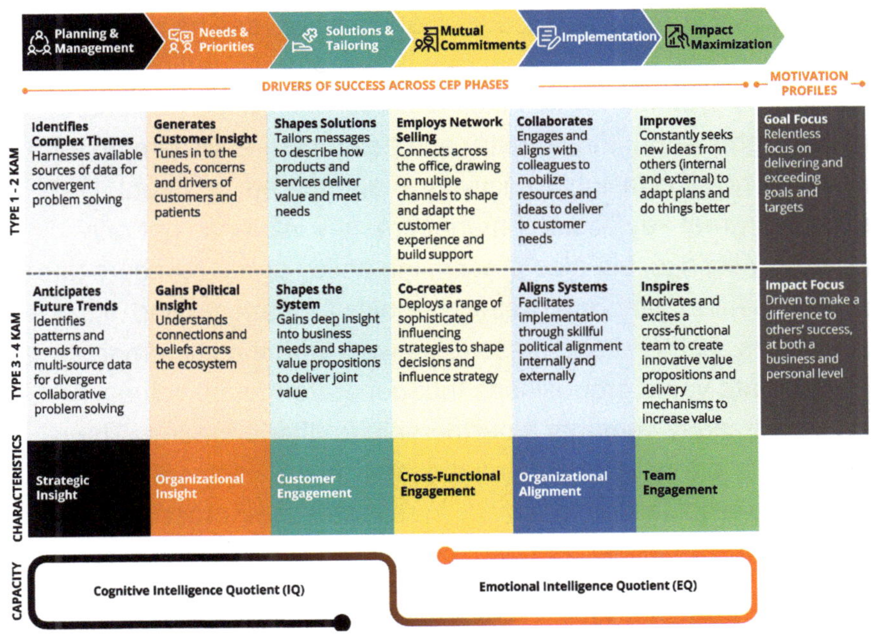

Figure 11.3 *Success drivers across the Customer Engagement Process (CEP).*

quarterbacking. In life sciences, these roles often concentrate on selling into hospitals or larger providers. The larger the customer, the more these roles need to understand and address customers' needs over the long term. In addition, they often need to bring a network-selling mindset to customer relationships, seeing them as part of a connected healthcare ecosystem and broadening their connections across the hospital. This requires more coordination, greater customer and business insight and the ability to wrap therapies or procedures, resources and services around these needs to deliver value to the customer. Compared with a specialist sales rep, these roles must be able to synthesize more complex information across organizations, people and value propositions. In addition, they need more sophisticated influencing skills and the ability to successfully mobilize cross-functional teams to collaborate and innovate to better meet customer needs.

In the more advanced Type 3 and Type 4 KAM models, the level of sophistication required in capabilities takes another leap forward. High performers in Type 3 and Type 4 KAM models practice highly complex account management, seeing themselves as advisors and influencers of both the customer and often the healthcare system in which the customer operates. They share their insights about the industry and healthcare environment and use their political insight to actively shape the environment. For example, great key account managers may influence not only formulary listings, but also prescribing policy or the reimbursement environment to generate greater benefits for patients and customers. At their best, these roles work with the customer to co-create value propositions that generate mutual value, which ultimately cements a partnership for the long term. They are equally adept at navigating the internal environment, using skillful stakeholder management to reinforce their organization's credibility as a partner for customer success.

Another insight on key account managers in Type 3 and Type 4 KAM models from our research stood out: In sourcing talent, organizations should look for people who are more impact-oriented than goal-oriented. Outstanding key account managers are energized by and find satisfaction in making a difference and having a positive impact on others (such as a customer's personal and business success or patient health outcomes). They also have a more holistic view of what success is, with a medium- to long-term horizon. Therefore, they're more likely to favor generating lasting mutual value over simply reaching immediate sales targets as their ultimate goal.

CONCLUDING THOUGHTS

While we've outlined some of the key factors that drive KAM success based on our research, it's critical that companies develop a full and customized competency model that's aligned to their unique objectives, value strategy, KAM model and customer engagement process. This focus ensures that the selection and development of talent reinforces the factors that will make the biggest difference in performance and drive the greatest value for the organization across the CEP. Aligning to the company's strategic objectives also emphasizes the importance of being future focused and highlighting competencies needed today and tomorrow.

Ultimately, the customers key account managers call on are among the most important for life sciences companies. These customers are complex and sophisticated, and to succeed, a company must put the right people with the right skill sets in front of them—it's too much of a risk not to. Frequently, this is not simply a matter of placing the best sales reps in the key account manager role—particularly given the large difference between these roles within life sciences. The value strategy, KAM model, customer engagement process, competency model, learning and development journeys, motivation systems and performance management systems all must be aligned to create a harmonious

KAM talent system where the pieces reinforce one another to benefit the customer, patients, the organization and the account managers themselves.

NOTE

1 John Hunter, Frank Schmidt and Michael Judiesch, "Individual Differences in Output as a Function of Job Complexity," Journal of Applied Psychology 75 (1990): 28–42, https://doi.org/10.1037/0021-9010.75.1.28.

CHAPTER TWELVE

The unique learning journey required for KAM

Chris Morgan, Tania Lennon and Namita Powers

As companies strive to develop the capabilities needed for effective key account management (KAM), training is usually high on the list. But the training required for the people involved in KAM is fundamentally different from, for example, training on a new product. Not only do companies need to convey new information, but they also must develop new thinking approaches and behaviors. And so, the approach to learning must be qualitatively different as well. In this chapter, we discuss the factors that influence KAM training and coaching, and the steps required for a successful KAM learning journey.

DOI: 10.4324/9781003226512-12

WHY IS KAM LEARNING UNIQUE?

As we noted in the preceding chapter, KAM success requires people with unique skills and characteristics as well as a very distinct way of engaging customers. As a result, a salesperson experienced in traditional selling methods targeted at individual physicians or surgeons won't necessarily be a high performer in a KAM model. This means the training and development that a company launching KAM puts in place must focus on developing the competencies, skills and behaviors that correlate with KAM success. Before discussing what this training and development looks like, let's touch on the three key factors that fundamentally require the key account manager learning journey to be unique.

First, **KAM is a team sport**. KAM stands for "key account management" first and only secondarily for "key account manager." Success in managing a key account depends on the effective coordinated participation of each team member touching that account. Roles that partner with the key account manager could include a sales representative who visits the department heads in addition to individual doctors; a medical specialist (whom we will refer to as an "MSL," although many names exist) who communicates with the chief medical officer and key opinion leaders; a marketing manager with product strategy expertise; a product or patient support specialist who has regular exposure to users' real-world issues; a business unit head brought in as a collaborative initiative's executive sponsor; and a host of other possibilities. KAM learning programs that focus exclusively on the key account manager role are inevitably destined to disappoint.

Second, **KAM competencies are adaptive**. The truly differentiating competencies that drive KAM performance are not predicated on simply executing a sequence: "Do A then B then

C." They are adaptive skills that require the team to interpret the account, the environment, the customers and the competition and decide how to adapt their strategies accordingly. As we discussed in prior chapters, examples of these competencies and where they manifest include:

- Providing consultative and trusted advisor insights
- Managing senior stakeholders across the decision journey
- Facilitating innovative solution-building across cross-functional teams
- Negotiating and structuring solutions to maximize joint value
- Orchestrating cross-functional implementation
- Identifying opportunities to maximize mutual value realization

Importantly, these competencies and behaviors share a key characteristic: They're all predicated on key account managers and their teams making good and consistent judgments. The difference between knowing the things you're supposed to do and being able to do them well is much greater than it is when learning the details of a new product. Most people in KAM organizations can tell you what templates or plans they're expected to fill out, but fewer are confident that they actually understand how to create the required inputs. The ability to make good judgments typically comes from time and experience, which leads us to the third point.

Third, **KAM is an apprenticed capability and takes practice**. Training has its place in developing KAM capabilities, but it's only the very beginning of the journey. Key account teams develop deep skills through continued and deliberate practice, with the support of someone who can challenge them, give them feedback and apprentice them.

The design of a KAM learning program needs to explicitly consider each of these distinctive factors.

DESIGNING THE KAM LEARNING JOURNEY

It's an all-too-common occurrence: A company launches a KAM program with a flurry of training activity. Team members enjoy the training—KAM is, after all, an exciting subject—and leave engaged and enthused. But somehow, six months later, the company sees no significant changes in behavior or impact (Figure 12.1).

Common feedback we hear from key account managers suggests some of the reasons why nothing really changes:

- "I understand the theory, but I'm struggling to relate it to the realities of our business."
- "I see how this works in high-tech or financial services, but I don't see how it works in healthcare."
- "I know what I'm supposed to do, but I don't know how."
- "I'm doing my best to change the approach, but other people in the organization don't seem to get it."
- "There's just so much to do. I'm being asked for 20 account plans, but the first one took me two weeks to write. I'm exhausted."

These critiques are all symptomatic of a training approach that hasn't embraced KAM's distinctive nature. To be successful,

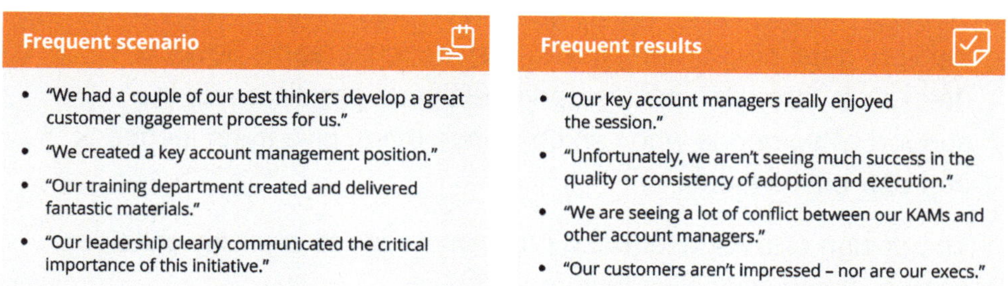

Figure 12.1 *The common approach to KAM training normally fails to achieve traction.*

KAM competency development must include several key elements:

- Developing "apprentice coaches" and enabling them to apprentice specific skills
  ... because KAM is an apprenticed capability
- Developing the account team together
  ... because KAM is a team sport
- Building adaptive competencies that are rooted in the customer engagement process (CEP)
  ... because the team needs to be able to exercise judgment in applying the CEP
- Practicing deliberately and making practice visible
  ... because KAM takes practice and the team needs to learn to adapt rather than to repeat a set formula

The "DATA" model in Figure 12.2 summarizes these ideas, which we'll explore in more depth in the remainder of this chapter. By design, these ideas overlap and co-mingle—for example, the purpose of an apprentice coach is to support deliberate practice. A good program design will therefore treat these as a system, rather than as separate items on a list to check off.

In the next section, we expand on the DATA model, starting with apprentice coaching and working to the left.

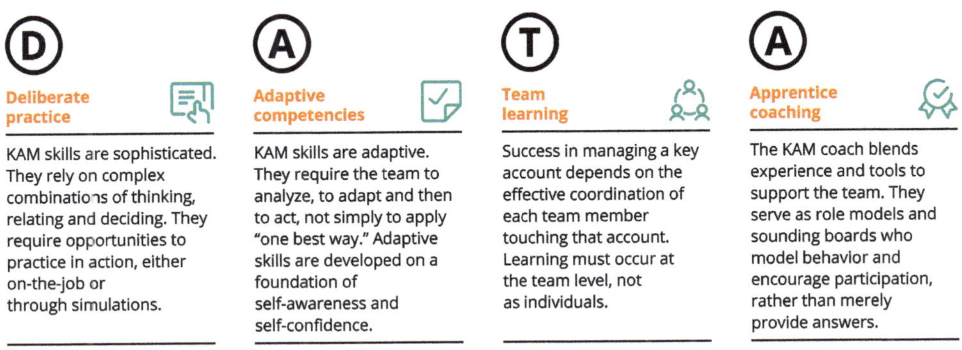

Figure 12.2 *The DATA model for developing KAM competencies.*

DEVELOPING APPRENTICE COACHES

Why do we use the term “apprentice coach?” How is it different from “just a coach”? Is the apprentice coach the same as a first-line manager or leader?

In the purest sense, coaching is agnostic of topic. Great coaches listen to people and, through questioning, enable them to discover answers for themselves, helping them develop the confidence to navigate uncertainty and change. A KAM coach needs these skills as well.

But when learning a completely new or elevated skill, it's also valuable to have access to a veteran who has experience solving similar problems before and can serve as an idea generator, a sounding board and a demonstrator of what success looks like. Otherwise, we're destined to discover everything ourselves through trial and error, which can be time-consuming and dangerous. Apprenticing electricians are rarely asked, “Why don't you try connecting that to the red wire and see what happens?”

An apprentice coach is a blend of these two things—someone who brings the experience and tools to help a team get started on new and unfamiliar problems but who doesn't just leap to providing solutions. The apprentice coach is an expert in the question, rather than simply a provider of answers, and can both reveal the path to success and demonstrate what good performance looks like along the way.

Ideally, first-line managers and leaders for KAM teams would both have the necessary skill set and play the role of the KAM apprentice coach. It's a critical part of the role. In some more constrained situations or market contexts, where first-line managers or leaders with KAM experience don't exist, it's important to identify someone in the broader organization who can play this apprentice coach role.

One particular challenge for life sciences manufacturers, however, is that KAM first-line managers may lack this skill set and there's rarely a pre-existing pool of people who have the perfect blend of experience, skills and availability to play this role to easily replace them with. Life sciences first-line managers with five to 10 years of KAM experience and good coaching skills are few and far between. So, companies must develop a pool of people to play this role, either by recruiting from outside the industry or developing their own people, both of which have their pros and cons:

- External recruitment
  - Pros: Quantity and quality of KAM experience; coaching skills; KAM credibility
  - Cons: Inexperience in healthcare and life sciences; difficult to attract; possibility of an organizational misfit; additional or replacement headcount
- Internal development
  - Pros: Knowledge of healthcare and the business; internal credibility; existing headcount; possible coaching skills
  - Cons: Inexperience in KAM; nature of established relationships; need to invest time to develop

For any apprentice coach, the role requires a set of attitudes, behaviors and competencies as described in Figure 12.3.

ENABLING THE ACCOUNT TEAM TO LEARN TOGETHER

Organizations commonly complain that team members drawn from different functions aren't working together effectively at key accounts. And yet, KAM training is frequently delivered exclusively to the account manager or, at best, delivered in silos to different functions—a huge missed opportunity. Teams are dramatically

Figure 12.3 *The profile of a good apprentice coach candidate.*

more effective if they actively think of themselves as a team, with their own set of team norms and practices.

KAM teams need to learn not only KAM ideas and principles, but also how the team best works together to deliver results. Clearly, a company should have a level of consistency in key processes (e.g., account planning and CEP), but teams need to find their own "style" based on their unique mix of personalities—from logistics, such as when and where to meet; to dynamics, such as who tends to frame the discussion, who challenges and who finds common ground.

Some key ideas to enable effective account team learning include:

Learn concepts in advance and practice in person. Time spent out of the field is a rare and valuable resource that should be used for the most impactful learning. For example, a lot of concepts are associated with effectively managing key accounts and whole books have been written on them. But these concepts can and should be absorbed before implementation through online media, making them available to team members at point of use. Since lectures on KAM theory may overwhelm the valuable time the team has together, companies should focus in-person or virtual sessions on the motivation for KAM and the application of concepts. Most key account managers and team members are better at acting themselves into a new way of thinking than thinking themselves into a new way of acting.

Practice application as a team. In the real world, KAM is executed by a team, so participants should practice not just in cross-functional workshop groups but with their actual account teams—the specific group of people with whom they will be working in the field. These training exercises enable participants to learn their particular role in, for example, understanding customer needs. They will also become more familiar with the roles played by other team members and how those roles interrelate. Figure 12.4 describes one such practice session.

Training program designers and leaders should be aware of two important qualifications:

- Not all topics are suitable for this approach. "Understanding customer needs" is a team responsibility and should involve team-based learning. In contrast, "Developing a contract," for instance, would probably be better if limited to the key

THE TEAM EXPERIENCE

A specialist pharma company was moving into a hospital setting and so launched a corresponding KAM program. The first major learning session brought the whole cross-functional account team (key account manager, field sales, medical and market access) together at one table, along with regional managers as coaches. Here's what some participants had to say:

"The most valuable thing about today was working together with my colleagues."

"Today I spent more time with my colleagues from other functions than I had in total in my career."

"It had never even occurred to me to ask what my medical colleague was trying to achieve in the account. I guess I've always thought of her as being there to do what I needed. That has totally changed."

Figure 12.4 *Experiences from a healthcare account team learning session.*

account manager and potentially legal, pricing or finance stakeholders.

- Some team members (e.g., MSLs) might work with multiple account teams. In these cases, it's helpful to seat the teams on adjacent tables (or the virtual equivalent) and have the shared team member move between their teams. This structure immediately simulates the real-life impact of competing demands for attention.

Explore mutual expectations. All teamwork is a matter of give and take. Each team member must understand that while they have their own objectives for the account and expectations of the other team members, the same is true for every other member of the team. It's important to spend time understanding everyone's objectives and mutual expectations.

Focus on the "how," not on the "what." No KAM program has succeeded because 10 extra templates were added to the training. More often the reverse is true. We've seen cumbersome programs collapse under the weight of dozens of different templates and highly successful programs that emphasized just a small number. Companies should focus teams on learning (a) the problem-solving and questioning approaches that can help them successfully develop account strategies; (b) the ability to critique and challenge the team's own ideas; and (c) the resourcefulness to find new ways to uncover information and deliver outcomes.

Make learning available at point of use. Account managers live in the field and encounter different situations and challenges every day. Not everything can be carried in one person's head until it's needed. In parallel with an integrated learning journey, KAM teams need access to fragments of learning that are available remotely and in real time.

Practice using real accounts. Pre-written, fictitious case studies are appealing because they give the facilitator a sense of control. But they also present two drawbacks for account teams: (a) because the case study will always feature details that differ from the team's own experience, participants can get bogged down by a sense that details are "unrealistic" when, in fact, they're just different; and (b) teams can feel like they're spending time working outside their business or "out of the field." To counter these drawbacks, companies should use a team's real-life account for practice wherever possible and have apprentice coaches facilitate and coach these sessions as a dry run for in-field practice.

BUILDING ADAPTIVE COMPETENCIES ROOTED IN A CUSTOMER ENGAGEMENT PROCESS

Any learning journey will, of course, include training as a core feature. While many KAM learning programs exist, we believe those rooted in a customer engagement process are the strongest and most intuitive for participants. Figure 12.5 gives an example of an integrated learning journey that's aligned to the CEP and includes the learning modules we believe are most impactful for a successful KAM learning program.

DELIBERATE PRACTICE IN THE FIELD

The final step in the KAM learning journey is to bring apprenticeship and team learning together. Real capability change is achieved when teams deliberately practice applying their learnings into their own business with the support of and feedback from their coach. Deliberate practice requires:

Intentionally scheduling time for deliberate practice. Look ahead at the account team calendar and systematically reserve time in

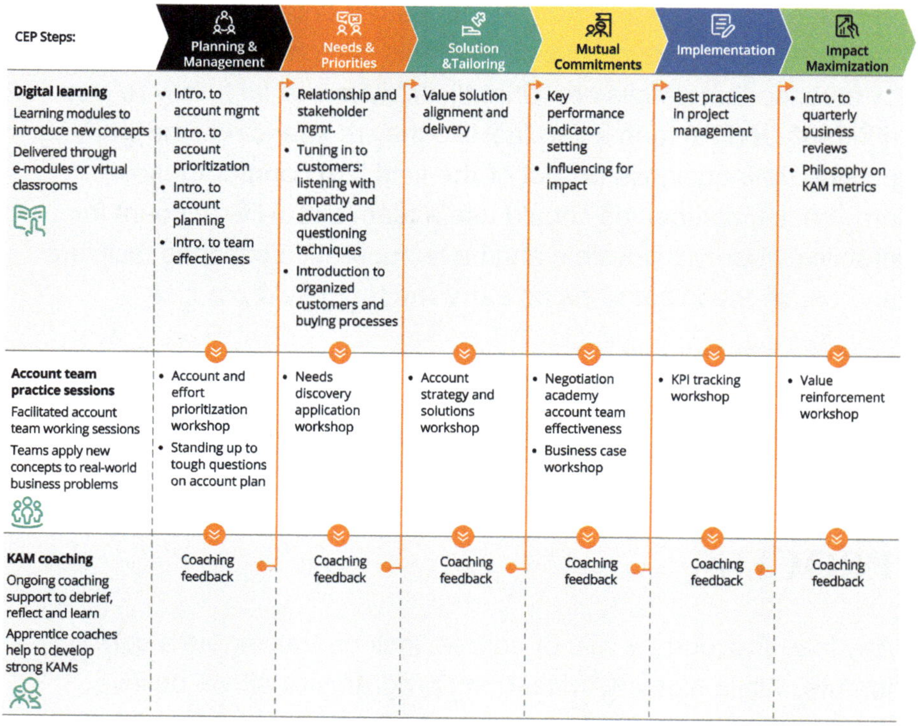

Figure 12.5 *Example integrated KAM learning journey for a cross-functional account team, aligned to the CEP.*

Note: The model also illustrates the multi-modal blend of online learning, account team workshops and in-field, coached, application and peer learning.

advance for practice. An ad hoc approach to practices generally means they likely won't happen. Initially, a once-a-month cadence is probably about right, depending on the timing of the selling cycle. Importantly, practice won't necessarily require additional time to be carved out: Pre-existing scheduled times—such as account team meetings or cycle meetings—can be re-purposed. And while the meeting's timing should be set in advance, each session's focus should be allowed to flex to match the current stage of the account's decision-making cycle. This helps forge a natural continuity with the business and from one session to the next.

Breaking the competency down. Coaches and their teams should focus on the relevant KAM skills for the current stage of the CEP. A key skill for coaches is the ability to identify which skill is useful and to sequence training and coaching accordingly. The biggest differentiator for top-performing account teams is their commitment to thinking and preparation between customer discussions, so KAM coaches should expect to spend most of their time coaching the thinking process rather than "in-call effectiveness."

Getting feedback and taking risks. Teams will only genuinely deepen their competencies if they attempt things they haven't successfully done in the past. If they've never done something, they need a coach to provide feedback, which must come without judgment. The only way to encourage team members to take the risks required for step-change growth is to create a safe environment in which trying and failing is accepted or even applauded.

CONCLUDING THOUGHTS

Patience and persistence are the final important ingredients for a successful KAM learning journey. Organizations that assume their KAM learning journey will be complete in six months are assuming the change required is small and will be universally and easily adopted. It isn't and it won't. The KAM programs that succeed understand that the road to success is permanently under construction. Only by creating the environment for teams to collectively try, fail, learn and grow will companies achieve true change and impact.

CHAPTER THIRTEEN

Key account manager incentive compensation: Aligning to strategic objectives

Subhashri Suresh, Tobi Laczkowski and Chad Albrecht

As key account management (KAM) becomes more important in life sciences and companies implement different KAM models, engaging and motivating key account teams has become critical to success.

KAM in life sciences is an organization-wide business strategy focused on developing deeper, mutually beneficial partnerships with important healthcare provider and payer systems and groups. The key account manager role is one element of KAM and is a substantially different role from field sales—which means key account managers require unique approaches to incentive compensation (IC) plan design. Unfortunately, many life sciences companies have relatively limited KAM experience and often apply

DOI: 10.4324/9781003226512-13

field sales compensation practices to the key account manager role. As a result, key account manager IC is often too focused on short-term demand generation and not enough on broader, longer-term KAM program objectives.

In this chapter, we introduce six guiding principles critical to designing and implementing an effective key account manager IC plan and share some best practices along the way.

GUIDING PRINCIPLE 1: DESIGN IC TO FIT THE PROGRAM OBJECTIVES; ONE SIZE DOESN'T FIT ALL

Throughout this book, we've discussed how KAM isn't a one-size-fits-all approach but, instead, comes in different forms, as depicted in Figure 13.1. Life sciences companies should employ appropriate flavors of KAM based on their business objectives

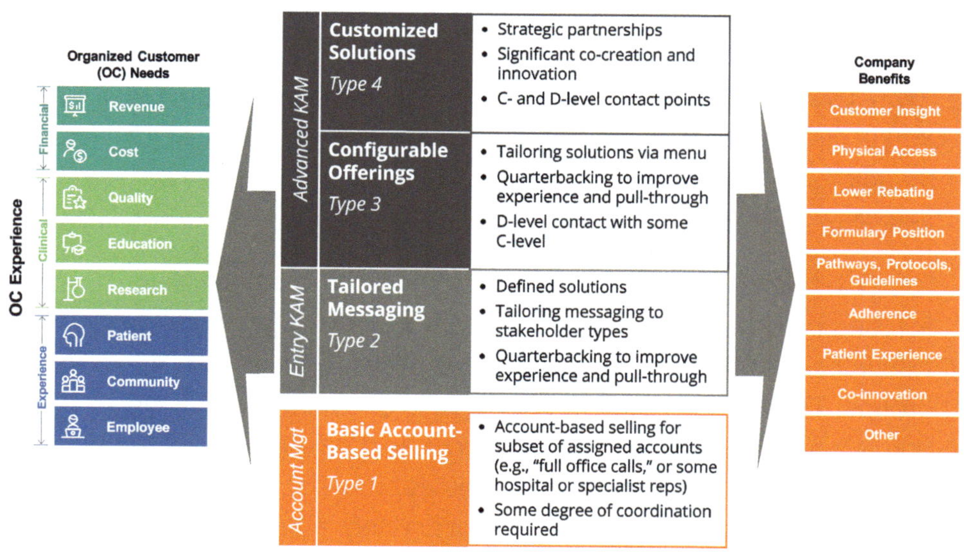

Figure 13.1 *KAM isn't one-size-fits-all.*

which, in turn, should influence how key account manager IC plans are designed.

For example, for most Type 1 models focused on basic account management and not generally considered KAM, IC plans that are tightly linked with the field sales organization tend to make sense. In these models, the account manager role is generally focused on basic account selling and coordinating selling efforts, so more traditional field sales IC plans can be effective. As we move to KAM, such as Type 2, and especially Type 3 and Type 4 KAM models, increasingly sophisticated IC plan design is warranted, taking into account the KAM organization's broader and longer-term goals. Such plans can include leading metrics, lagging metrics, voice of the customer (VOC) metrics and even shared outcomes that are mutually pursued with customers. In many cases, a management by objectives (MBOs) approach is used to incorporate leading metrics into the IC plan (which we'll discuss shortly).

Incentive plan metrics should follow closely from the specific business objectives the organization wants to achieve through KAM. This alignment requires a cascade. Business objectives are translated into the program metrics that will be used to assess and manage the KAM strategy's overall impact. Program metrics are then translated into individual metrics that will be used to track and manage individual key account manager performance. Finally, a subset of individual metrics is selected to be incorporated into the key account manager IC plan. This sequence is illustrated in Figure 13.2.

Ultimately, the metrics selected for the key account manager IC plan must tie directly to the business objectives KAM is designed to help the company accomplish. While those objectives vary by organization, typical ones in life sciences tend to be associated with some or all of the following:

- Primary point of contact to orchestrate internal coordination and drive customer experience

- Advanced solutions to improve clinical, financial, patient experience and employee experience outcomes
- Formulary access and position; product access
- Clinical and operational protocols and procedures
- Basic contracting (based on volume, etc.)
- Product bundling (cross-business unit or enterprise-wide)
- Sales representative access to physicians (maintain or increase)
- Innovative contracts (based on value, indication or outcomes)

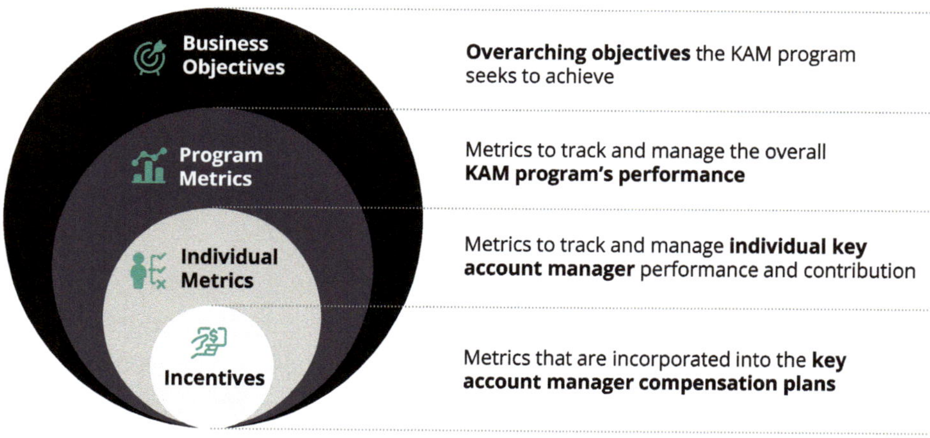

Figure 13.2 *Key account manager incentive plan metrics link back to KAM business objectives.*

GUIDING PRINCIPLE 2: BALANCE THE USE OF LEADING AND LAGGING METRICS FOR HOLISTIC INCENTIVES DESIGN

As discussed in our chapter on KAM metrics, individual key account manager metrics fall into one of four categories (as depicted in Figure 13.3): leading, lagging, VOC or shared outcomes.

Leading Indicators

- Customer insight
- Account plans
- Decision maker engagement
- Top-to-tops
- Needs validation meetings
- Business case reviews
- Joint planning and investments
- Relationship strength
- Program "traction metrics"
- New programs
- Innovations
- Clinician access
- Formulary, pathway and protocol
- New RWE partnerships

Voice of the Customer

- Net promoter
- Customer satisfaction

Shared Outcomes

- Patient education
- Health economics and outcomes research
- Adherence
- Disease management
- Quality of life

Lagging Indicators

- Patient volume
- Sales and share
  - By clinician
  - By center or system
- Platform penetration (cross-sell)
- Profitability
- ROI
- Growth

Figure 13.3 *KAM requires a balanced scorecard, comprising leading and lagging metrics.*

Designing the right mix of IC plan metrics is critical to achieving the longer-term focus required to maximize KAM's impact. Unfortunately, many key account manager IC plans in life sciences tend to be based heavily on lagging metrics that inadvertently drive a short-term focus. KAM's intent is to develop deeper and more strategic partnerships that result in greater benefits to both organizations. In many cases, the programs and initiatives that key account teams want to execute with organized customers require long cycle times, often extending beyond a single fiscal period. Plans that overemphasize lagging metrics motivate the development of transactional relationships that undermine the pursuit of these longer-term, higher-impact solutions and partnerships.

As a result, leading metrics play a critical role in key account manager IC plans. Leading metrics are used to measure and reward progress against objectives with longer time horizons. A combination of lagging and leading IC metrics balances accountability for outcomes while recognizing and rewarding success in achieving key milestones tied to longer-term initiatives.

Leading metrics also help focus attention on the levers that individual key account managers most directly influence—recognizing that lagging metrics are strongly influenced by many customer-facing roles.

Selecting the right leading metrics for the IC plan can be challenging given the range of possibilities, behavioral implications and measurability requirements. Here are four considerations.

1. Fewer metrics in key account manager IC plans is often better, with four being the most that should be used. Too many plan metrics reduce the importance of any one component and invariably undermine the plan's impact. The IC plan is important, but it's not the only way organizations motivate the desired behaviors and manage performance.
2. Quality is always more important than quantity, and binary "yes versus no" activity metrics should be avoided. For example, the quality of quarterly business reviews (QBRs) would be a much better metric than the number of QBRs.
3. The best leading metrics are those that are the most predictive of likely outcomes. For instance, a leading metric tied to achieving key new partnership milestones might be more predictive of future outcomes than a metric tied to account plan quality.
4. Leading metrics can change over time as the KAM program evolves. For instance, activity-based metrics such as "number of key decision influencer calls" might be used in the early stages, whereas "relationship strength by influencer" might be used as the KAM capability matures.

In addition to leading and lagging metrics, VOC and shared metrics are also options for key account manager IC plans. Net promoter score[1] (NPS) is a common VOC metric, but other customer experience and customer satisfaction metrics are also possible. VOC metrics can be very helpful as inputs in coaching key account managers. That said, the verdict is still out regarding incorporating them into key account manager IC plans. There are two main concerns:

1. Tying key account manager IC to customer experience scores can inadvertently motivate price discounting and other forms of value giveaways.
2. Ongoing customer experience tracking in business-to-business selling environments is more challenging than for individual clinicians, and life sciences in general is still early in the journey of developing this capability.

Organizations that choose to incorporate VOC into the key account manager IC plan must establish robust VOC tracking platforms and implement guardrails that protect against unintended behaviors. These guardrails could include internal checks and balances or lagging metrics that reinforce desired pricing and mutual benefits.

Incorporating “shared outcomes” is less common for key account manager IC plans, but some leading-practice KAM organizations have done it. Shared outcomes are performance metrics that typically link to the achievement of the customer’s objectives. The power of including these in a key account manager IC plan is that they reinforce the organization’s commitment to the customer’s success. Key account managers with such plans have even gone as far as communicating to their customer that they’re personally evaluated based on how well the customer achieves its objectives.

The relative weighting of leading metrics and lagging metrics often shifts over time as the KAM program matures. But organizations should always strive for a healthy combination of both leading and lagging metrics, often with each representing approximately 40% to 60% of target incentives (Figure 13.4).

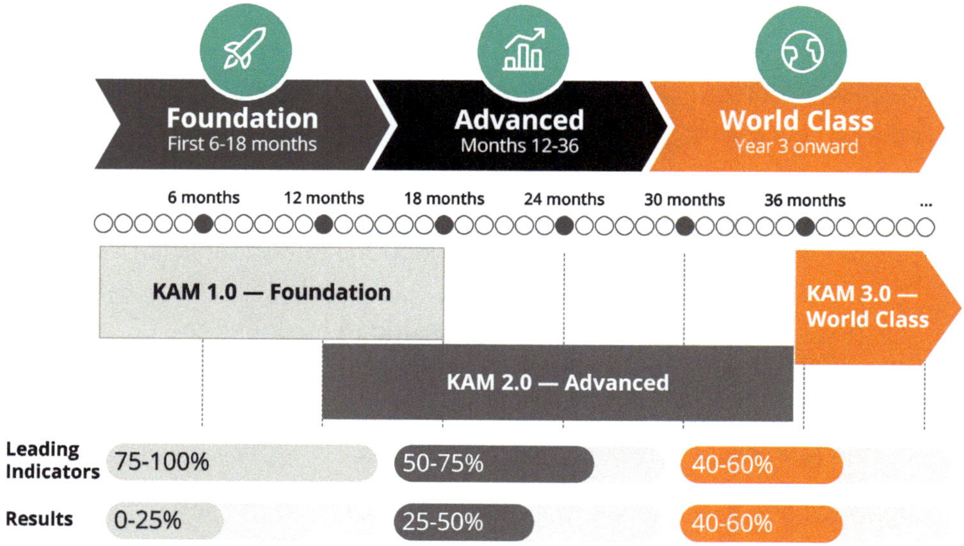

Figure 13.4 *The mix of leading and lagging metrics shifts over time.*

GUIDING PRINCIPLE 3: GET COMFORTABLE WITH A HIGHER SALARY MIX AND USING NONTRADITIONAL DATA FOR INCENTIVES MEASUREMENT

Relative to the rest of the sales force, key account managers should have a different target mix of salary versus incentives that results in less at-risk pay. This is due to the following factors:

- More executive nature of the key account manager's role
- Longer-term nature of business objectives
- Less precise measurement data available for organized customers

As a result of these factors, in life sciences, salary plays a bigger role in the typical key account manager salary-to-incentive mix than it does for the rest of the sales force. For example, if a given company has a sales force with a target of 70% salary and 30% incentives, then key account managers might have a target of approximately 80% salary and 20% incentives. In this example, the 20% weighting is still significant enough to affect behaviors yet reflects the key account manager role in a more appropriate, less transactional way.

Organizations should keep an open mind when it comes to the nature of the data to inform incentives for key account managers. For many leading metrics (e.g., quality of account plans, decision-maker engagement or relationship strength), the data will likely include inputs from managers and, in some cases, may even be self-reported. This can still be leveraged for IC as long as a well-defined quality control mechanism is in place. For instance, a reasonable process could include having individual key account managers record stakeholder mapping and relationship strength in a central system, then reviewing those inputs regularly with the managers in ongoing check-ins to verify progress and maintain process integrity. These are common practices in other industries.

GUIDING PRINCIPLE 4: DESIGN IN OBJECTIVITY, EVEN FOR "SOFTER" METRICS

The use of MBOs is a common practice in key account manager IC. MBOs are closely associated with one or a combination of leading metrics and are used to describe the degree of attainment relative to objective, specific, and observable behaviors and accomplishments. When designed effectively, they can be a powerful element of a key account manager IC plan. But when designed poorly, they can become a glorified "check the box" exercise and, in a sense, become hidden salary.

MBOs shouldn't default to a yes/no (did/didn't achieve) measurement scale. Rather, MBOs should incorporate a grading scale of performance. These can include definitions of both quality and quantity and will bring much sharper accountability to the key account manager team. Even the softest elements can often be defined using detailed enough descriptors to identify relative degrees of success and outcomes. For example, a company that wanted to incorporate the completion of QBRs as an MBO could imagine replacing this one:

- Complete QBRs with each of your top three accounts

with this one:

- Number of mutual value-creation initiatives, worth at least $1 million in revenue each, agreed in writing with your top three accounts during QBRs and acted upon by the end of the quarter

In the above example, a sliding scale could be designed to pay the target amount based on the target number of initiatives and would pay more or less based on the actual performance.

ZS's MBO design framework, IMPACT, can be a useful tool for designing a holistic and well-functioning MBO program with actionable and purposeful MBOs based on observable behaviors and outcomes (Figure 13.5):

Figure 13.5 *A well-designed MBO program goes beyond objective setting.*

This intentional approach helps ensure the objectives:

- Are individualized and drive accountability
- Are limited in number with meaningful weighting
- Have a rating mechanism (like the sliding scale example) that allows the differentiation of top performers
- Emphasize quality of outcomes by being actionable and purposeful
- Are communicated and tracked clearly on an ongoing basis

GUIDING PRINCIPLE 5: ALIGN MOTIVATION SYSTEMS ACROSS THE ORGANIZATION

Up to this point, we have discussed the design of the key account manager IC plan. What about the IC plan for roles that team up with the key account manager to serve these accounts? KAM typically requires teamwork across many different customer-facing roles, each of which often reports to different leaders and parts of the organization. Examples in life sciences include sales representatives, medical science liaisons (MSLs), health economics and outcomes researchers (HEORs), product specialists, clinical specialists, field marketing personnel and many others. The question is to what degree these other roles should be evaluated against the same metrics as the key account manager and whether a team-based incentive should be put in place.

Harmonizing individual metrics across customer-facing roles is essential. If team members have directly conflicting metrics and motivation systems, the team is set up for destructive tension and poor results. But that doesn't automatically mean a team-based IC element is required. At minimum, individual metrics for each role need to be aligned to the same set of fundamental objectives as the key account manager metrics. But different roles have different functions and may warrant different metrics. For instance, the "number of potential investigators identified" might be an important metric for an MSL but may not be appropriate for a key account manager or sales representative. In addition, legal and regulatory considerations preclude certain metrics from being applied to medical roles. Thus, harmonization of the metrics across coordinating roles—not standardization—is the goal.

Taking the next step to team-based incentives is a complex decision and is only effective in select circumstances. A number of factors must be considered including the following:

- **Alignment of customers and accounts.** Team incentives work best when the key account manager and associated team members are highly aligned to the same system of providers or payers. If there's not enough overlap, it's difficult to justify a meaningful weighting to the team component for roles that have the more diverse responsibilities.
- **Ability to link individual physician performance with overall system performance.** Many life sciences companies are still working toward the ability to roll up individual physician performance to individual organized customers based on affiliations. This capability is required to measure an individual salesperson's contribution to an organized customer's results.
- **Relative contribution of each role to the team metric.** If some roles have dramatically more influence over the attainment of the team metric than others, lower-impact roles will tend to experience windfall gains or losses that aren't in their control.
- **"Free-rider" concerns.** Top performers often worry they will be pulled down by lower performers or low performers will unfairly benefit from their contributions.
- **Lack of incentive plan.** Not all customer-facing roles in life sciences warrant a variable incentive plan, and legal and regulatory considerations influence which types of metrics and plans are appropriate for specific roles.

All these factors need to be carefully assessed when evaluating the pros and cons of team-based incentives. In many cases, the answer will be to harmonize metrics and then look to other drivers beyond incentives to motivate and enable teamwork. These include a well-defined customer engagement process and operating model, tools and processes for account planning and coordination, metrics for both the program and the individuals that track coordination quality beyond the IC plan and strong senior executive alignment and support.

GUIDING PRINCIPLE 6: COMMUNICATE BROADLY TO DRIVE ORGANIZATION-WIDE UNDERSTANDING AND SUPPORT

Communication strategy and rollout is an especially important aspect of a key account manager IC plan's success. Companies that do this well plan for it at the initial stages of the IC plan design process. Identifying and onboarding some field champions in the design process, and eventually during plan rollout, helps drive broader field buy-in.

The degree of detail communicated should be enough to explain the objectives and highlights, yet spare the detailed analysis leading up to it. For key account manager IC plans in particular, the role's influence can span multiple product lines or even business units. The associated stakeholders should also get some education on the basics of the key account manager IC plans. The communication should reinforce the tangible ways in which the KAM strategy and the key account managers will help the organization achieve its objectives.

Ideally, the key account manager IC plans are communicated at the same time and venue as the rest of the field IC plans. It's an excellent opportunity to communicate a cohesive strategy across the organization. When done well, this aligns cross-divisional leadership and fosters buy-in with the broader field stakeholders.

CASE STUDY: MEDICAL PRODUCTS KAM TEAM IC PLAN OVERHAUL

Now let's look at a case example of a multidivisional capital and consumable medical products company that incorporates many of the leading practices we've highlighted and demonstrates the criticality of getting the key account manager IC plan right.

KAM strategy and challenges: A cross-divisional KAM organization wasn't seen as adding value and sometimes was viewed as detracting from the divisional ability and agility to develop and execute effective contracts. Divisional leaders resented the "KAM tax" that each had to pay to fund the KAM organization, while the relationship between the key account manager role and the divisional sales teams was ambiguous and key account managers weren't emphasizing some parts of the portfolio. Not surprisingly, a significant proportion of the key account managers had low morale and lacked motivation.

Existing IC plan: The plan in place was heavily weighted toward short-term sales targets and simplistic MBOs, including number of contracts signed without consideration of quality and scale. Incentives also existed for number of QBRs with targeted accounts but had no regard for quality or impact.

Approach: With C-suite endorsement, the KAM leader formed a core team including members from each division, plus central functions such as finance. C-suite personnel committed their time for oversight and to reflect the importance of KAM to the organization.

The team went through a comprehensive process of benchmarking, external customer research, internal divisional feedback, historical analytics and forward-looking scenario planning to create a new IC plan that reflected organizational priorities and made the key account managers significantly more accountable.

KEY ASPECTS OF THE UPDATED IC PLAN

- Redesigned and reduced weighting on **lagging** metrics
  - Result: A portfolio revenue metric with extra emphasis on longer sales cycle products to align with the company's priorities
- Redesigned and increased weighting on **leading** metrics
  - Result: A contract signing metric with stepwise payouts per contract based on the number of strategic attributes included in the contract
  - Result: A customer engagement metric that provided multiple opportunities to earn based on a calibrated points system where points earned are based on NPS, development of joint customer initiatives and execution of customer contract elements

KEY BENEFITS OF THE REDESIGNED IC PLAN

- Differentiates high performers from low ones via increased slope of payout accelerators
- Provides the opportunity for overachievement on each metric
- Reduces the lag between activities and payouts for most metrics
- Allows leadership to place the appropriate levels of emphasis on core objectives and communicate clear links between the company strategy and key account manager performance
- Removes check-the-box elements
- Takes advantage of both internal and external benchmarks to optimize and incorporate overall best practices, salary-to-incentives target mix and payout period

Impact: The IC plan played a major role in this organization's larger transformation and was credited with delivering significant impact—accelerating growth in key accounts faster than in non-key accounts. The new design brought consistency and mutual understanding across the organization and resulted in increased accountability, mutual value creation, shared understanding and improved outcomes. Also, previously underperforming product lines got more attention and began growing, consistent with the key account manager IC plan emphasis. Internal respect for key account manager value increased dramatically.

CONCLUDING THOUGHTS

As demonstrated by the preceding example, key account manager IC plans can have a significant impact on company performance. The best key account manager IC plans are aligned with the KAM strategy and objectives, strike the right balance between leading and lagging metrics, ensure objective assessment of both quality and impact, reflect longer-term time horizons, and are well communicated and understood by all stakeholders. By following the six guiding principles we discussed, organizations can create a more motivated and accountable key account team, more strategic and meaningful engagement with key customers and better organization-wide alignment and support.

NOTE

1 Net promoter score (NPS) is defined as the fraction of customers rating themselves as promoters (score of 9–10) minus the fraction rating themselves as detractors (score of 0–6) to the question "How likely would you be to recommend [x] to a friend or colleague?" on a 10-point scale, ranging from 0 (not at all likely) to 10 (extremely likely).

CHAPTER FOURTEEN

Why technology is critical for breathing life into KAM

Ankit Jain, Mike Powers and Pratap Khedkar

Key account management (KAM) continues to develop as a critical business strategy for life sciences companies seeking to differentiate themselves and to create stronger customer value in an increasingly competitive marketplace. And as a comprehensive go-to-market strategy, not just a role within a field sales organization, KAM requires the participation of people in a wide range of company functions—something life sciences companies increasingly recognize.

During a 2021 ZS roundtable that included 17 industry leaders representing 10 life sciences organizations, nearly all participants identified their primary KAM challenge as being able to work as an organization in a coordinated, collaborative and cross-functional way. In other words, the primary challenge isn't limited to the KAM strategy itself, but is also focused on the strategy's execution. Companies recognize that effectively bringing together the people

DOI: 10.4324/9781003226512-14

and processes to execute KAM across the entire organization plays a key role in unlocking the KAM go-to-market strategy's value.

One of the biggest drivers of such collaboration is technology. Technology enablement and analytics-driven decision-making can and should be an engine for breaking down cross-functional silos and effectively executing a KAM strategy. Yet, time and again, we see companies choosing to deprioritize investments in KAM technology and analytics or not fully recognizing them as complementary to existing commercial technology priorities. Case in point: In two recent research studies, "State of KAM in Pharma," and "State of KAM in Medtech,"[1] only one-third of participants identified technology and analytics as a top investment priority critical to advancing their KAM strategies.

In this chapter, we discuss common KAM technology challenges and how life sciences organizations can maximize KAM technology and analytics investments to drive higher value and impact with their most important customers.

WHY SHOULD LIFE SCIENCES ORGANIZATIONS PRIORITIZE INVESTMENTS IN KAM TECHNOLOGY AND ANALYTICS?

Technology and analytics are critical to KAM success for several reasons. First and foremost, KAM represents a significantly different go-to-market model from the traditional one-to-one promotional selling model that's powered the life sciences industry for decades. KAM is focused on identifying and addressing the needs and priorities of a much broader and diverse set of key decision influencers in large and complex systems—and seeks to provide advanced solutions that go well beyond the customer needs addressed by core products such as pills, medical devices

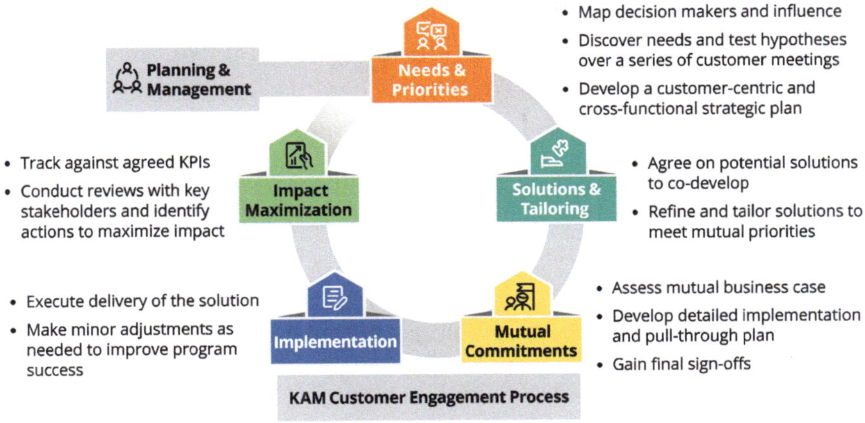

Figure 14.1 *The KAM customer engagement process.*

and medical supplies. Furthermore, as described in Chapter 9, the customer engagement process required to achieve these objectives is substantially more complex than the traditional one-to-one selling model. Figure 14.1 provides an example of the phases typically associated with a KAM customer engagement process along with each phase's underlying objectives.

Four factors specific to the KAM customer engagement process require companies to invest in advanced technologies beyond the typical one-to-one selling models life sciences companies use:

1. KAM is a "team sport." KAM requires a coordinated approach to customer engagement, insights and measurement across many functional roles. For instance, in the life sciences industry, this may include marketing, market access, Health Economics & Outcome Research (HEOR), patient support, field sales and the account managers themselves. Traditional sales automation tools used in life sciences often don't support KAM sufficiently because they were built with only field sales roles in mind. They can't drive coordination, collaboration and pull-through across all these functional groups as they navigate the key account customer engagement process.

2. KAM is focused on identifying and tailoring “advanced solutions” (such as programs, services and systems) that meet the higher-order needs of complex and strategically important organized customers. Promotional materials developed for one-to-one selling fall dramatically short of enabling this capability. KAM requires more sophisticated technology, including account-based marketing capabilities that give key account managers access to configurable solutions, value-in-use calculators and messaging.
3. KAM requires deep insight into customer needs and opportunities. In addition to primary marketing research and account team insight, customer-focused key performance indicators (KPIs) help diagnose customer opportunities. As a result, high-performing KAM organizations complement their internal performance analytics with KPIs and analytics focused on understanding their customer’s business performance. This outside-in thinking represents another significant shift from traditional life sciences selling models that drives the need for a new approach to customer analytics.
4. KAM requires a “balanced scorecard” to both evaluate program impact and manage performance more broadly. KAM dashboards must have the right mix of leading and lagging metrics based on strategic objectives and the KAM program’s overall maturity. Tracking these metrics requires new data sources and new ways of capturing and validating key inputs.

In short, investments in technology and analytics can improve the KAM customer engagement process in several important ways. These include fostering a better understanding of customer needs, tailoring and communicating advanced solutions and associated value propositions, collaborating cross-functionally on business planning and customer engagement, identifying customer opportunities through KPIs and tracking KAM program impact on those KPIs.

WHAT ARE THE MOST COMMON KAM TECHNOLOGY CHALLENGES?

In the past few years, we've seen several life sciences companies pursue technology and analytics investments to enable their KAM business model, with limited success. These initiatives have been plagued by a pattern of start-stop efforts, myriad overlapping technologies that aren't fit for purpose and a lack of a clear vision of the full suite of digital technology and analytics capabilities required to enable KAM. The following three technology challenges occur most commonly in KAM.

1. **Filling gaps via point solutions instead of building capabilities incrementally and aligned to a holistic vision of the data, technology and analytics capabilities required to enable KAM**. Common statements such as "we need a new account planning tool" and "we need an account master data management (MDM) solution" hint at a limited focus on the overall digital capabilities required for KAM. Integrating these point solutions into the existing technology infrastructure frequently proves to be challenging and costly.

   Systems and processes often need to be re-wired multiple times when these systems are incrementally and individually deployed. A more holistic and long-term vision of the capabilities required to support KAM can enable better planning and coordination across the enterprise and help minimize technical debt by synchronizing deployment plans across the data, technology and analytics ecosystem.

2. **Trying to fit a square peg in a round hole by repurposing tools built to support the traditional one-to-one promotional selling model**. The analytics, data and systems used for decades to support the traditional physician promotional selling model has limited applicability to the KAM business model.

Attempts to repurpose these capabilities, such as traditional sales automation platforms, often create more burden than benefit for key account managers who are asked to use tools that don't meet their needs. Furthermore, these solutions often ignore the technology and analytics needs of other internal stakeholders such as marketing and HEOR, who play key roles in enabling the KAM business model. As a result, we consistently see key account managers and other stakeholders reverting to old ways of working, often with offline tools and frameworks built in Excel and PowerPoint that significantly limit the organization's ability to collaborate on key account plans and initiatives and institutionalize KAM learnings.

3. **Limiting KAM-relevant insights and analytics to traditional data sources and not focusing on developing a proprietary data strategy for the organization's most important customers.** Deep customer insights are important to life sciences organizations' ability to create differentiated value for their customers, yet organizations often try to leverage standard data sets known to the industry at large to develop such customer insights. We see companies struggling to determine key customer insights such as the degree of control exerted in the provider's local market or even basic insights such as provider organization intent as implied by KPIs related to rep access, net promoter score and key clinical pathways. Leveraging standard data sets to understand how sophisticated customers operate and what they care about can be too tall an order. Life sciences companies need to become more comfortable with exploring and even creating new data via multiple channels such as field intelligence, unstructured data from digital sources, voice-of-the-customer research and other real-world data sets. Shifting focus from internal analytics such as product volume and share to externally focused analytics, which are KPIs that matter to the customer, will become a key differentiator for forward-thinking life sciences companies.

Ultimately, a more focused effort on developing organizationally exclusive data with a deeper richness of insights about the organization's most important customers will lead to the competitive differentiation the KAM business model can foster.

HOW CAN LIFE SCIENCES ORGANIZATIONS MAXIMIZE KAM TECHNOLOGY AND ANALYTICS INVESTMENTS?

KAM requires a high degree of cross-functional coordination, collaboration and agility, with technology playing an important role in removing the biggest barrier, siloed ways of working. Life sciences companies therefore need to ensure they adopt the right technology to support their KAM strategy across the Understand-Communicate-Collaborate-Measure framework, which ideally uses fit-for-purpose platforms. Figure 14.2 illustrates four key areas of focus.

Figure 14.2 *Four opportunities to enable KAM customer engagement via technology and analytics.*

1. **Understand: Build strong foundational organized customer data and insight capabilities.** Leveraging data and analytics to understand and uncover deep customer insights provides a foundation to any KAM capability and often acts as the first step of a KAM technology roadmap. A variety of emerging, niche and disparate data sources are required to achieve a deep understanding of the complex multi-layered organized customers that exist within healthcare. Furthermore, KAM fundamentally requires multiple internal functions working together to support the engagement process, making it essential to provide a consistent yet tailored version of account hierarchies, structures and profiles across these functions. Three areas are critical early steps in building out a robust KAM data and insights capability:

   - **Organized customer master data management**—While different functions will need multiple views of the same account or system of accounts, building a centralized and single master version of the truth will enable downstream analytical consumption methods like KAM dashboards and insights tools.
   - **Organized customer 360**—This capability enables a life sciences organization to know its account, its business and local market dynamics. An account 360 provides a comprehensive view of all the touchpoints and interactions, both internal and external, across all customers, and enables analytics across functions covering key decision makers, affiliations, account hierarchies, key influencers and others.
   - **KAM analytics modules**—These ensure the technology architecture is future-proof to enable new types of analytics. As the KAM strategy matures, the need for analytics will evolve from basic to sophisticated, such as developing an advanced understanding of an IDN's

intricate care network, its healthcare objectives and priorities, its key decision makers and its presence and influence in local markets. An organization should develop a variety of analytics capabilities, including KAM scorecards, performance dashboards and next-best action capabilities using artificial intelligence and machine learning, as well as local market insight tools. In doing so, the organization should adopt a mindset that sits at the intersection of analytics and technology, or AnalyTech, to both execute complex analytics to answer key business questions and leverage technology to ensure that capability can be scaled across the organization.

2. **Communicate: Enable account-based marketing as a mission-critical capability.** B2B leaders recognize a well-functioning KAM strategy drives profitability and growth. They also understand the criticality that KAM-specific marketing plays in defining and enabling an effective KAM strategy. As a result, account-based marketing programs continue to grow, fueled by the delivery of strong results, including higher account engagement, improved win rates, larger average deal size and strong ROI. Other B2B industries are already leading the trend by leveraging technologies to prioritize key accounts, creating contacts and mapping to the accounts, creating account-specific content and messaging, and managing and orchestrating account engagement across channels.

3. **Collaborate: Enable collaboration across the organization and within account teams via fit-for-purpose account planning and management tools**. Best-in-class account planning and management combines rich customer insight, deep strategic thinking, cross-functional collaboration and disciplined preparation. Plus, it isn't purely defined by the end document. Today's best-in-class account planning and management platforms are broad enough to include all

relevant organizational functions and can enable a wider set of KAM capabilities. These platforms often include several forward-thinking capabilities life sciences companies can take advantage of as they continue to build and advance their overall KAM capabilities:

- **Customer value creation playbooks** help teams discover their customers' needs, align those needs with mutual opportunities and guide teams on how to implement solutions.
- **Advanced solution repositories** allow marketing and KAM teams to articulate the customer benefits that can be achieved via the advanced solution services, programs and systems that key account teams can tailor with their customers.
- **Customer impact quantification tools** compliantly estimate the business impact the life sciences company's advanced solutions can achieve for its organized customers.
- **Cross-functional engagement collaboration capabilities** remove silos by ensuring teams constantly update one another on plan execution progress and work together to adapt the plan as they learn more through their customer engagements.
- **Seamless integration capabilities** across the customer relationship management, reporting and analytics and marketing automation platform ecosystem help enable KAM at scale.

4. **Measure: Develop KAM-centric scorecards to effectively track key measures of success.** Enabling a KAM strategy requires a comprehensive performance measurement capable of both continuously communicating the value of the KAM business model and motivating the organization to achieve the desired outcomes. By first establishing a

KAM KPI framework focused on leading indicators, lagging indicators, shared outcomes and VOC metrics, life sciences organizations can align on what defines success for the KAM program, both internally and with key account customers. As one can imagine, aligning on these KPIs can be challenging, but technology ramifications for enabling KAM scorecards often get overlooked. Specifically:

- A wide variety of disparate data sources will need to be analyzed for KAM KPI calculations. Third-party, first-party, field-generated and other internal data sources will likely be required for KAM scorecards.
- The quality of the KAM KPI data sources can vary significantly, requiring a major focus on data quality management frameworks and techniques as part of the scorecard development.
- The KAM organization will continuously evolve, thereby requiring changes to the KAM KPI framework over time. Depending on the KAM program's maturity, the metrics most critical to focus on at a given point in the KAM journey will be different. Consistent governance on and refinements to the KAM KPI definitions and the KAM scorecard are essential.
- Different stakeholders will need different KAM scorecards and views. Analyzing local market insights for opportunities, KAM program performance, key account performance and pull-through analysis requires focusing on different personas and how the scorecard will be used by each to support their various decisions and actions.

CONCLUDING THOUGHTS

In the early days of KAM in life sciences, when organizations typically saw KAM as a role, it was easy to anchor on enhancing the skills of the field-based account managers. But as KAM has become increasingly understood as an organization-wide business strategy, life sciences organizations must do far more. They need technology to operationalize and scale the model, as well as manage the complexity that comes with the increasingly cross-functional engagement and collaboration needed to make the model successful. Significant revenue and growth opportunities await leading-edge life sciences companies willing to commit to the technology and analytics investments required to drive higher value and impact with their most important customers.

NOTE

1 ZS and Strategic Account Management Association, "State of Key Account Management in Pharma" and "State of Key Account Management in Medtech," Q4 2020.

CHAPTER FIFTEEN

KAM in the United States versus Europe: Are we headed to the same place?

Falko Graf-Meisner and Chris Morgan

Key account management (KAM) has become an important topic for life sciences companies in both the United States and Europe. As organized customers rise on both sides of the Atlantic, decision-making is becoming more complex and decision power is shifting away from the individual doctor. The COVID-19 pandemic also accelerated the driving forces behind KAM, including provider re-organization and regional differentiation. Companies in both geographies must continue to invest in KAM to remain relevant for patients, providers and payers. There are differences between KAM in the United States and Europe, and companies need to be aware of them as they continue building their global KAM standards across or within their therapeutic areas or service lines. But those differences shouldn't blind us to the

DOI: 10.4324/9781003226512-15

similarities. Understanding both the differences and similarities is key to defining globally consistent KAM standards while allowing for locally relevant execution. While we talk about Europe in this chapter as though it's one entity, this is clearly a simplification because there are many nuances across the region's healthcare systems, geographies, languages, economics and cultures.

In this chapter, we briefly review the evolution of healthcare systems in both geographies and explore the impact on global KAM development and local KAM implementation.

COMING FROM DIFFERENT STARTING POINTS, EUROPEAN AND U.S. HEALTHCARE SYSTEMS ARE NOW CONVERGING

Most European healthcare systems trace their roots to the Bismarck model, developed roughly 150 years ago by the Prussian chancellor and based on the concept of solidarity, equality and social responsibility. In contrast, the U.S. free-market-like healthcare system evolved in line with the socioeconomic concepts of Adam Smith, who believed a competitive market would significantly benefit society. Those distinct concepts behind European and U.S. healthcare systems drive significant differences in funding, access and government intervention (Table 15.1).

The opposing origins of the European and U.S. healthcare systems created two different market archetypes. European markets established hierarchical market structures in which national and subnational organizations provide regulating frameworks under which regional and local organized providers operate. Additionally, most European citizens have always had access to publicly funded healthcare. In the United States, the healthcare market is fragmented and divided between competing provider and payer organizations. Only a subset of the U.S. population has

Table 15.1 *Bismarck versus Smith—the origin of today's healthcare systems in Europe and the United States*

Europe—Solidarity-based concept of healthcare	United States—"Free market"-based concept of healthcare
• Social redistribution of income and resources to ensure broad and free access to healthcare. • Free choice and use of healthcare. • Highly regulated healthcare frameworks and public funding to prevent system failure.	• Funding and healthcare provision through the public sector, with private insurance options at various levels, co-pays and deductibles. • Limited choice in a defined system, with not all citizens having access to publicly funded care. • No significant intervention by the government; healthcare providers and insurance companies regulate prices and service levels.

been covered by publicly funded healthcare, as most healthcare spending comes mainly from the private sector (Figure 15.1).

Now, systems on both sides face the same challenges of an aging population, combined with an increasing prevalence of chronic diseases. At the same time, the pool of healthcare talent is decreasing and labor cost is rising. These challenges accelerate the evolution of healthcare systems and the convergence of the

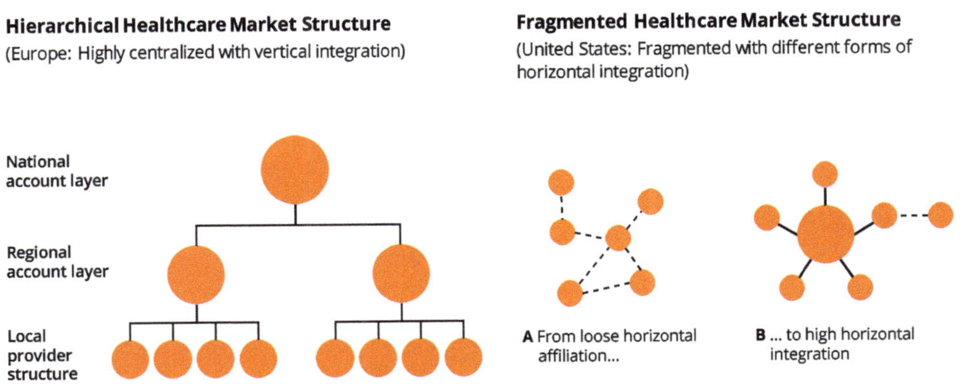

Figure 15.1 *Healthcare market archetypes in Europe and the United States.*

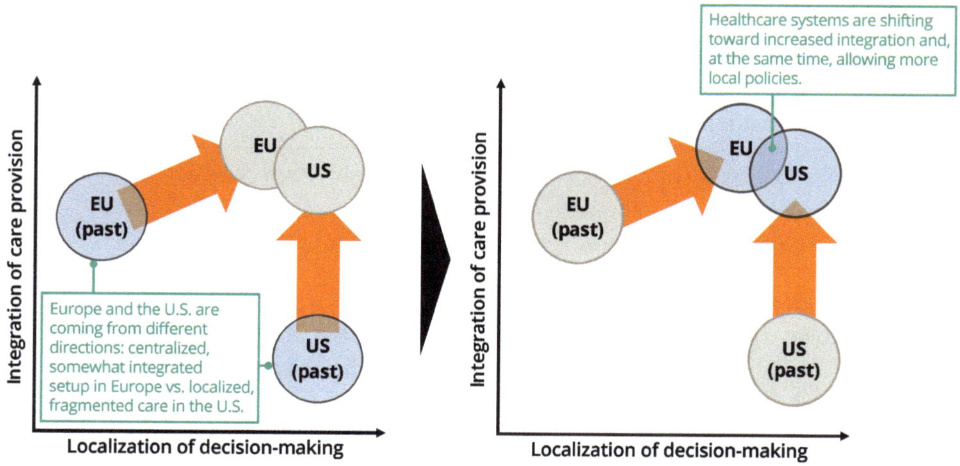

Figure 15.2 *European and U.S. healthcare systems are converging.*

European and U.S. models (Figure 15.2). This "hybrid model" features vertical integration in healthcare provision and allows certain free market mechanisms at the local level to deliver tailored care to a locally defined patient population.

One can't assume universal healthcare provision in a controlled market will equally benefit the whole patient population. European markets are learning location matters—the socioeconomic profile determines the healthcare environment (Table 15.2).

Table 15.2 *Example of regional socioeconomic and healthcare differences in Europe*

	Bavaria	Lower Saxony	North Rhine Westphalia	Saxony
Socioeconomic environment				
Inhabitants '000 (2018)	13,077	7,982	17,933	4,078
Capita per km^2 (2019)	185	167	526	221
GDP EUR per capita (2019)	48,323	38,423	39,678	31,453
Unemployment rate (2019)	3.8%	6.0%	7.7%	6.4%
Healthcare infrastructure				
Capita per physician (2019)	200	238	207	224
Capita per hospital bed (2018)	172	190	150	155
Public hospital investment (EUR per bed, 2018)	8,261	6,169	4,482	4,176

Source: Federal Statistical Office Germany, Federal Medical Association, Germany.

Devolving power and horizontal integration in European healthcare markets

United Kingdom: According to NHSCC, Clinical Commissioning Groups replaced the Primary Care Trust in 2013 and, since then, became responsible for the planning and commissioning of health care provision for their local area. They cover approximately two-thirds of the total NHS England budget.

Germany: More than one-third of all physicians work in a healthcare network that aims to connect general practitioners and specialists with different institutional partners, such as nursing homes, hospitals and patient associations.

Sweden: Healthcare funding and provision is decentralized to 21 county councils that are self-governing and empowered to align healthcare operations to local conditions. Approximately 90% of county spending is on healthcare.

Figure 15.3 *Examples of increasing localization in European healthcare systems.*
Sources: https://sweden.se/life/society/healthcare-in-sweden, maintained and operated by the Swedish Institute (SI); https://www.arztnetze.info/, maintained and operated by Agentur Deutscher Arztnetze e.V.; https://www.england.nhs.uk/commissioning/, maintained and operated by NHS England.

Because European countries require strategies that ensure equal healthcare opportunities and support local patient needs, many devolve power to the local healthcare structure and continue to drive vertical integration (Figure 15.3).

The U.S. healthcare system is fragmented for patients, providers and payers. Localized healthcare provision has always been the case, with local healthcare providers having significant local influence. This led to inefficient care coordination and resource allocation. To improve quality and outcomes, as well as reduce costs, those inefficiencies must be eliminated. Therefore, organized customers have been evolving in the United States, such as integrated delivery networks (IDNs) that are consolidating healthcare providers and exerting greater control over healthcare provision. The same trend can also be seen with payer organizations.

KAM IS EXPECTED TO DRIVE ORGANIC GROWTH IN THE UNITED STATES AND EUROPE, BUT ONE SIZE DOES NOT FIT ALL

The need to build stronger local networks within a more controlled integrated environment requires life sciences companies in the

United States and Europe to evolve their KAM strategies in a similar way to help them navigate the complexities of increasing localization and integration in healthcare. To achieve excellence in KAM, these companies will need to:

- Gain leadership commitment to overcome inertia embedded in existing strategies
- Elevate tactical planning skills to strategic business planning for organized customers
- Build and strengthen KAM capabilities across functions
- Focus on value-based account engagement and integrated customer experiences
- Develop innovative and differentiated solutions that address key account priorities
- Shift from a rigid reporting structure to flexible operating models
- Measure the mutual impact for provider, payer, patient and company

While KAM's driving forces and overall approach are consistent across the United States and Europe, local implementation differences exist. Three fundamental differences, in particular, affect local implementation of global KAM standards.

1. CAPABILITY BUILDING: THE CLOSENESS OF COMMERCIAL CAREER PATHS IN EUROPE FACILITATES INTERNAL KAM CAPABILITY BUILDING

U.S. and European leaders recognize capability building as a priority to accelerate KAM. The cross-functional nature of KAM capability building makes these intentions particularly challenging.

European customer-facing organizations are smaller than those in the United States, driving the emergence of hybrid or single roles with broader responsibilities, while in the United States, we see a trend toward an increasing variety of specialist roles.

For Europe, this means commercial career paths are more similar to each other and there's likely to be greater overlap in skills and competencies among roles. Thus, the step from demand-generating, brand-focused roles such as specialty care sales representative to value-generating, strategy-focused roles such as key account manager is smaller than in the United States. In Europe, cross-functional KAM teams are easier to develop from the internal talent pool because individuals have a higher chance of experiencing or at least observing the desired responsibilities.

On the other hand, the lower population in Europe limits the available talent pool in a given country and affects the scalability of global or regional talent management programs. Different local European labor laws further add to the complexity of requirements for successful talent management in Europe.

The different starting point for KAM talent development underpins the importance of global KAM standards. Life sciences companies define KAM-specific competency models that help to understand local starting points and to build KAM development centers with locally tailored solutions for talent identification, as well as individual and team KAM capability building.

2. VALUE STRATEGY: KAM ORGANIZATIONS ARE WORKING WITH DIFFERENT REQUIREMENTS TO CREATE AND CAPTURE HEALTHCARE VALUE IN EUROPE AND THE UNITED STATES

Because the healthcare supply chain is a cost center for provider organizations in the United States and Europe, optimal allocation of resources is key to efficient healthcare provision. The goal behind resource allocation and utilization differs significantly between the United States and Europe and affects the way KAM can create value for providers, payers and patients.

In the United States, individual eligibility for insurance coverage and the desire to optimize local services based on patients' affordability and willingness to co-pay drive care provision. In the absence of explicit coordination among providers, this creates competition for patients at the local level. Providers capture value by attracting the optimal patient population for which cost-effective care solutions are available and affordable. The goal behind resource allocation, then, is to match the services on offer to patients' differing needs and preferences.

In Europe, healthcare providers typically operate with a fixed patient population, balancing the need to provide equitable access to improved quality of care with the need to ensure cost-effective care provision. Although patients in Europe are free to choose their provider, competition among providers is limited by selection of third-party payers and their willingness to finance provider offers. In addition, the concept of universal healthcare coverage in Europe reduces the attractiveness of out-of-pocket payment solutions.

A primary focus of value creation through KAM on both sides of the Atlantic is cost reduction and outcome improvement. KAM organizations in the United States aim to help local healthcare providers attract the optimal case mix to maximize revenues and optimize the delivery of care at defined points in the patient journey for which profitable solutions are available. At the same time, payers and providers are increasingly looking to collaborate to achieve more profitable healthcare delivery and better patient outcomes. Additionally, patient satisfaction, the third key player, grows with the type of services and care directly received, which means service improvements and the overall patient experience are important value drivers.

European KAM organizations look to help providers optimize care delivery for a defined case mix and seek solutions to reduce the costs of healthcare provision. Patient satisfaction and experience with the overall healthcare system is seen as more important to driving quality and care improvements across the integrated healthcare provision chain. Providers are looking for solutions that consider the entire patient journey and benefit the entire patient population.

However, with the increasing integration of healthcare in the United States and the partial localization in Europe, KAM value strategies are going to pursue similar objectives and both geographies can learn from each other. The United States is likely to adopt the concept of allocative value aiming for equal and cost-effective resource allocation across the care continuum. European healthcare systems must allow more local empowerment and regulated competition in care provision. Global inventories of account needs and associated value solutions can facilitate experience exchange and drive KAM transformation.

3. OPERATING MODEL: U.S. KAM ORGANIZATIONS ARE MOVING TOWARD LOCALLY TAILORED OPERATING MODELS, WHILE THE EUROPEAN OPERATING MODEL REQUIRES LESS LOCAL VARIABILITY

The definition of the appropriate operating model depends on the market architecture. The hierarchical structure in Europe provides clear guidance on which types of teams are needed to cover which account layers, and how they need to interact. There's limited local variability and a certain level of vertical integration. KAM organizations that operate in countries with a higher degree of vertical integration, such as the United Kingdom, Spain and Germany, establish regional, subnational and national key account teams in addition to local account teams to effectively influence decision-making across the entire healthcare system. Vertical integration also results in greater overlap between account teams in a given country. The integrated top-down policy making drives less variability in the role mix for KAM teams because the needs of account customers within an account layer are driven by the same regulating forces.

The localized structure in the United States drives toward tailored operating models and cross-functional team composition focusing on local provider and patient needs. The localized setup and the higher variability in role specialization mean less overlap among account teams, and the role mix among those teams can differ significantly depending on the required local KAM capabilities.

Life sciences companies have developed and introduced decision aids in the form of market archetypes or decision frameworks to help the United States and Europe identify the appropriate operating model based on an understanding of prioritized account layers, account intent and needs and required supporting KAM capabilities.

CONCLUDING THOUGHTS

As the U.S. and European healthcare systems both continue to evolve toward increased vertical and horizontal integration, the need becomes more pronounced for KAM as a business strategy to successfully navigate complexities. Commonalities in the driving forces behind KAM are enabling companies to more efficiently define global KAM standards, but the different origins of healthcare systems in the United States and Europe created important disparities that still affect the local implementation of KAM capability building, value strategy and operating models. Understanding and effectively accounting for these differences will help life sciences companies ultimately translate global KAM standards into locally efficient KAM approaches that can help them achieve their growth ambitions.

CHAPTER SIXTEEN

The future of KAM in life sciences

Mike Moorman, Namita Powers, Joe Stevens and Rohan Agni

The rise of organized customers—large, sophisticated and complex healthcare provider and payer systems and groups—has dramatically elevated KAM's importance for many life sciences companies. In landmark state-of-KAM in pharmaceutical and medtech research studies[1] conducted by ZS in partnership with the Strategic Account Management Association, greater than 90% of U.S. KAM leaders indicated their senior-most executives view KAM as a strategic priority. But this same study also underscored that the industry is at a relatively early state of KAM effectiveness.

Organized customer trends and KAM's current state in life sciences raises three questions about the future of KAM in the industry: How will the importance of KAM evolve in life sciences? In what ways will organizations seek to advance their KAM strategies and capabilities? How might longer-term shifts in the healthcare ecosystem and priorities impact KAM?

DOI: 10.4324/9781003226512-16

In this final chapter, we provide some perspectives on these three questions.

CUSTOMER TRENDS POINT TOWARD KAM BECOMING INCREASINGLY IMPORTANT

Three primary factors are dictating the degree to which life sciences companies are prioritizing KAM as a business strategy:

1. The relative size of organized customers and the overall market share they represent
2. The degree of centralized decision-making by organized customers—coupled with the control they can exert over individual clinician product choice and life sciences company interactions
3. The mutual benefits life sciences companies can realize by helping organized customers achieve their broader clinical, financial, patient experience and healthcare provider work life objectives

Trends related to these factors vary by therapeutic area and service line and, as a result, impact life sciences companies differently based on portfolio. But the bigger picture is clear: KAM will become an increasingly important strategy and capability in the years ahead for many life sciences companies. Consider the following trends that are playing out in the U.S. health system:

1. **Increasing size and dominance:** Horizontal and vertical consolidation continues to increase organized customers' size and dominance. On the provider side, health systems have been consistently consolidating for more than a decade. This trend continued in the first half of 2021, undeterred by the COVID-19 pandemic, with transacted revenue reaching

$8.5 billion, the second-highest total in the past five years.[2] For pharmaceuticals, the top three pharmacy benefit managers (PBMs) now process 77% of all relevant drug claims, and the top six PBMs process 95%.[3] Furthermore, the percentage of physicians now fully employed by large health systems or corporate entities continues to grow rapidly, increasing from 38% in 2018 to 53% in 2020.[4]

2. **Increasing centralized decision-making and control:** Organized customers continue to increase centralized decision-making and control over clinician prescribing and product choice decisions. In a 2020 survey, 86% of integrated delivery network (IDN) administrators reported they believe centralized decision-making and control will continue to grow. For pharmaceutical products, 77% of provider organizations now track drug utilization using "physician scorecards," with one in three tying scorecard performance to physician compensation.[5] Payers are also making their power felt, evidenced by the yearly increase of excluded drugs in the formulary of major PBMs.[6] For medtech products, 78% of IDN administrators indicated they employ value analysis committees to drive product choice at their organization.[7] Furthermore, payer pressure and consumer choice are driving patients to alternate sites of care (ambulatory surgery centers, urgent care clinics, skilled nursing facilities, home health agencies, etc.), often owned by chains that exert control and top-down decision-making.
3. **Decreasing sales rep access:** Organized customers continue to reduce life sciences company access to individual physicians. Sales representative access to individual physicians has been on the decline for more than a decade, with some specialties, like oncology, experiencing some form of access restrictions on up to 73% of their physicians.[8] Access during the COVID-19 pandemic dropped to near zero and has only bounced back to 70% of pre-pandemic levels, 20% of which is now virtual. Even when access returned,

many institutions began deploying appointment systems or administrative staff that act as gatekeepers, which reduces achievable visit frequency.[9]

4. **Increasing interest in partnering:** Organized customers continue to pursue clinical, financial, patient experience and staff experience objectives that require solutions beyond basic pharmaceutical or medtech products. At the same time, innovations in data, analytics and digital technologies are increasing the ways in which life sciences companies can help providers and payers address these objectives. As a result, organized customers increasingly are demonstrating willingness, ability and interest when it comes to partnering with life sciences in a range of areas as exemplified in Figure 16.1 for provider organizations.
5. **Increasing evidence of mutual benefits:** KAM is generating positive benefits for organized customers and life sciences companies alike. Organized customer administrators historically have been skeptical of life sciences because of a perceived misalignment of goals. For example, sales representatives are sometimes viewed by administrators as being solely focused on sales and market share, while health system executives are

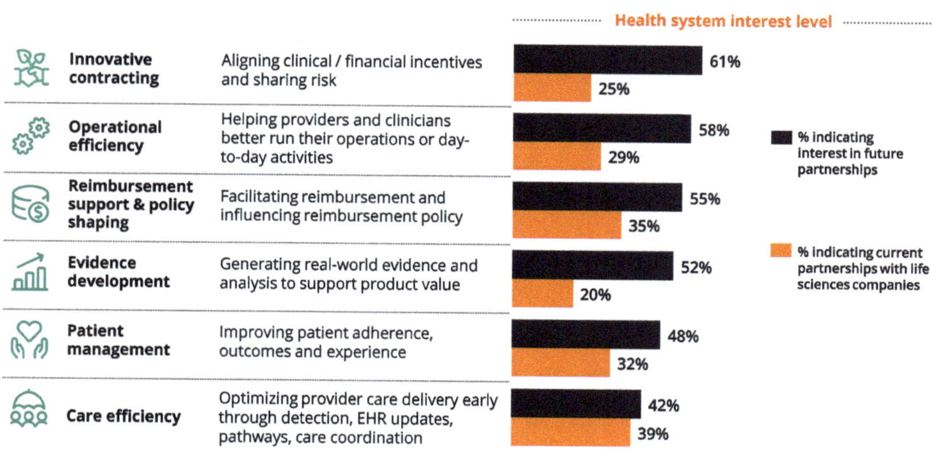

Figure 16.1 *Provider organization interest in partnering with life sciences.*
Note: Results are aggregated across therapeutic areas and service lines.

more worried about clinical outcomes, the patient experience and controlling costs—different objectives that can directly conflict. As manufacturers have begun to implement KAM, as well as think beyond their core offerings and develop advanced solutions focused on improving care in their therapy area or service line more generally, mutual goals have become more clearly aligned, benefitting both the customer and life sciences companies. For instance, our customer research has found a strong correlation between an organized customer's net promoter score (NPS)[10] for pharmaceutical companies and the number of advanced solutions each customer participates in with that company (Figure 16.2).

In combination, these five trends provide a compelling case for the escalating importance of KAM in life sciences. This is especially true for life sciences companies that compete in therapeutic areas and service lines that receive a higher degree of administrative attention and control. For instance, three therapeutic areas currently attract the highest degree of administrative scrutiny of

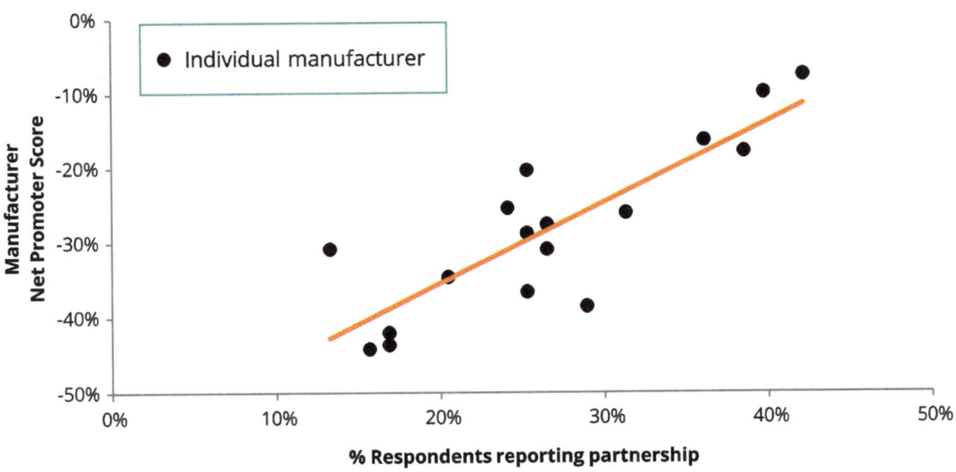

Figure 16.2 *Manufacturer NPS increases with the number of advanced solutions deployed.*

Source: ZS, "Provider Organization Partnership Tracker Wave 2" study, July 2019.

pharmaceutical product usage as a result of patient population sizes, treatment costs and potential to improve on clinical, financial and experience outcomes: oncology, cardiovascular disease and infectious disease.[11] On the medical device side, large capital equipment and vascular surgery products are two examples of areas receiving a high degree of management attention—and often fierce price competition between manufacturers.

It's important to realize that customers, not manufacturers, will dictate the future of KAM in life sciences. Organized customers' growing size, increasingly centralized control, evolving needs and changing partnership preferences will motivate manufacturers to adopt increasingly sophisticated levels of KAM. Given current trends, not only is KAM in life sciences here to stay, but it will also become even more important in the days ahead.

KAM IN LIFE SCIENCES IS MOVING TOWARD ADVANCED SOLUTIONS AND ENGAGEMENT MODELS

Insights from the ZS and Strategic Account Management Association studies[12] on the state of KAM in pharma and medtech provide an important perspective on the ways in which KAM will likely evolve in the industry. These studies were groundbreaking in their depth and breadth—addressing objectives, organization design, operating models, supporting functions, current effectiveness, barriers, metrics and investment priorities. Participants included 34 leaders of KAM functions spanning enterprise and business unit KAM organizations at 25 leading life sciences manufacturers. Together, the participating companies represented half of "big pharma" and the majority of major medtech companies.

Two results from this research are particularly revealing in terms of KAM's future direction in life sciences:

1. KAM effectiveness in life sciences is still at a relatively early stage, with significant advancements still required to achieve stated objectives and desired outcomes.
2. Future investment priorities in life sciences strongly point toward increasingly sophisticated KAM strategies and capabilities focused on providing advanced solutions tailored to individual organized customers.

We explore these insights and their implications in the following sections.

LIFE SCIENCES IS CURRENTLY AT AN EARLY STAGE OF KAM EFFECTIVENESS

KAM is still a relatively new strategy in life sciences, with many organizations having launched their KAM programs in just the past few years. While life sciences has made impressive strides in KAM in a short period of time, the industry overall is at an early stage of KAM effectiveness. Figure 16.3 provides aggregate scores for each of the KAM360™ effectiveness drivers sorted from highest to lowest effectiveness.

These results are encouraging because they imply that for each of the KAM360™ drivers, there are examples in life sciences of highly effective KAM programs. At the same time, these scores clearly show that life sciences is still early on its KAM journey. Of the 16 drivers, only key account selection and deselection was given a “high effectiveness” rating by half or more of pharmaceutical or medtech companies. And the drivers associated with more advanced KAM strategies and capabilities—such as value proposition and solutions, customer engagement process and operating model, and account-based marketing—received very few to no high effectiveness ratings.

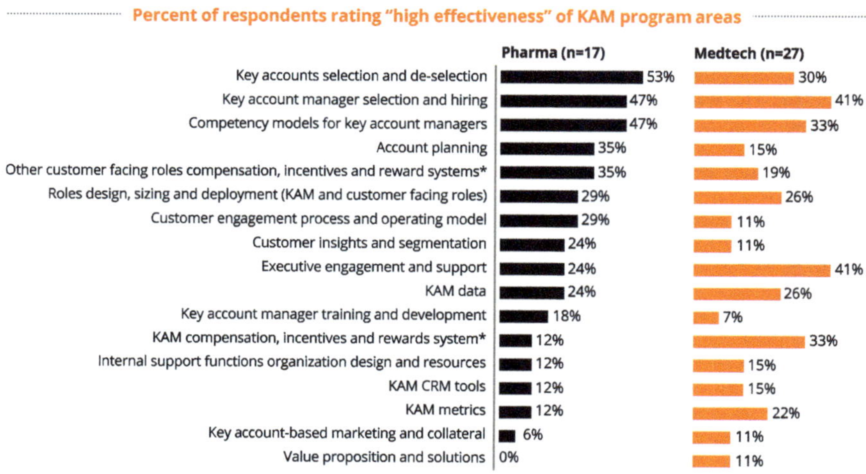

Figure 16.3 *"High effectiveness" ratings by KAM360™ driver.*

Note: Relative to the KAM360™ framework, compensation has been broken out into individual subcategories for key account managers and other customer-facing roles.

Together, these results suggest that most life sciences organizations have achieved a basic level of KAM but have yet to evolve to the more advanced KAM strategies and capabilities required for tailored solutions, strategic partnerships and broader mutual impact. This latter point becomes particularly relevant given the key objectives organizations identified for their KAM initiatives, as shown in Figure 16.4.

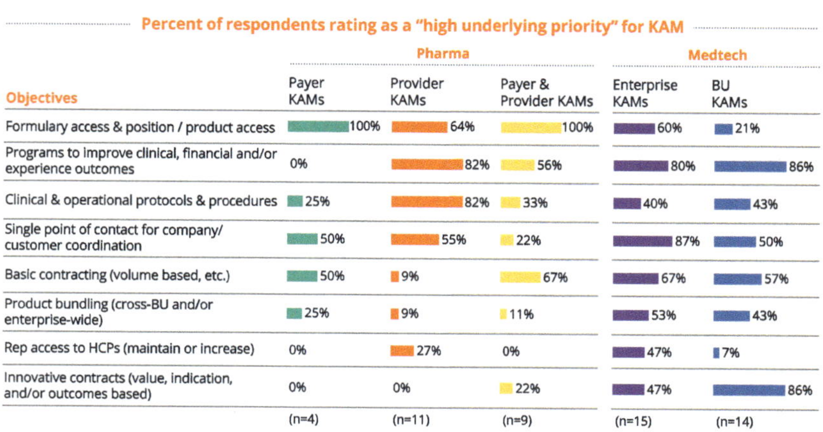

Figure 16.4 *Top objectives by type of KAM.*

Objectives such as "programs to improve clinical, financial and/or experience outcomes" and "innovative contracts" require effectiveness in precisely the drivers that many in the industry rate as ineffective. This brings us to future investment priorities for KAM in life sciences.

THE NEXT GENERATION OF KAM IN LIFE SCIENCES WILL INCORPORATE ADVANCED SOLUTIONS AND CAPABILITIES

KAM-related investment priorities for any company should be influenced by current effectiveness but also investment-level requirements, likely business impact, interdependencies, feasibility and time horizons. It's not just about improving; it's about getting better in ways that will generate the greatest outcomes.

The future investment priorities indicated by KAM leaders in U.S. life sciences paint a picture of an industry that's on the path toward capabilities that rival those of world-class KAM organizations in any industry. Figure 16.5 provides the percentage of respondents who rated each of the KAM360™ drivers as a top investment priority for their organization.

The most prevalent KAM-related investment priorities are nearly the same for the pharmaceutical and medtech sectors, which share a similar set of organized customers. Of particular note: **Value proposition and solutions** is the most frequently cited investment priority in both pharma and medtech. This imperative directly aligns with organized customer interest in partnerships and with the opportunity for life sciences companies to impact broader clinical, financial and experience outcomes in ways that benefit both organizations. Both pharma and medtech will need to invest in segment- and account-based marketing to develop and scale advanced solutions and value propositions. For example, only one-third of medtech companies currently have marketing

KAM360™ Driver (n=17 respondents)	% Respondents rating as high investment priority: Pharma	Medtech
Value proposition and solutions	59%	70%
Roles design, sizing and deployment	53%	48%
Key account manager training and development	47%	48%
KAM metrics	47%	19%
Customer engagement process and operating model	47%	56%
Key account manager selection and hiring	47%	26%
KAM data	35%	33%
Account planning	35%	44%
KAM CRM tools	35%	30%
Internal support functions organization design and resources	29%	41%
Executive engagement and support	29%	37%
Key account-based marketing and collateral	24%	26%
Customer insights and segmentation	24%	48%
Key accounts selection and de-selection	24%	15%
Competency models for key account managers	12%	15%
Other customer facing roles compensation and rewards*	12%	4%
KAM compensation, incentives and rewards system*	6%	7%

Top
Middle
Bottom
Top Overlap

Figure 16.5 *Investment priorities by KAM360™ driver.*
Note: Relative to the KAM360™ framework, compensation has been broken out into individual subcategories for key account managers and other customer-facing roles.

support beyond traditional brand and product marketing.[13] Misalignment between enterprise-to-business-unit or business-unit-to-business-unit value propositions was also highlighted as a top barrier to effectiveness. New forms of marketing and cross-functional support will be required to develop deep organized customer insight, segment-specific advanced solutions and value propositions, and supporting collateral and assets that KAM teams can leverage and tailor for individual key accounts.

Customer engagement process (CEP) and operating model (OM) is a close second as an investment priority for both pharmaceutical and medtech companies. Cross-functional organization-wide alignment is a major challenge in any industry, and life sciences is no exception. Life sciences' brand-centric planning processes and strong cross-functional and business unit silos were noted as key barriers to KAM effectiveness.[14] **Role clarity**, which has a strong interrelationship with CEP and OM, also stood out as a top investment priority. And the industry is still learning how to engage large, complex customers in ways that result in tailored solutions that motivate these customers to action. Innovation in CEPs and OMs, and the ways in which both are institutionalized, will be required to introduce the new types of advanced solutions and value propositions that both pharmaceutical and medtech leaders are prioritizing.

KAM training and development rounds out the top investment priorities shared by both pharmaceutical and medtech leaders. Life sciences leaders have clearly recognized the knowledge and skills required to be an effective key account manager are substantially different from those required to be a hospital or physician salesperson. Life sciences companies are beginning to develop more sophisticated competency models that align with KAM strategy and reflect research specific to life sciences KAM.[15] They're also looking beyond traditional sales as a source of talent. As the industry now makes the transition from basic KAM to advanced solutions and associated CEPs, new competencies and forms of training and development will be required.

The three investment priorities identified by the majority of life sciences leaders form a tight system. A shift to tailored value propositions and solutions requires new CEPs and OMs which, in turn, require new knowledge and skills. The three priorities in combination foreshadow a transition to more sophisticated KAM strategies and capabilities in the industry.

At the same time, many other KAM360™ drivers were selected as top investment priorities by some leaders. For example, roughly one-third of leaders view data, systems and tools as their top investment priority for KAM. And each of the 16 drivers was identified as the top investment priority by at least one organization. In the next several years, we expect to see greater industry-wide effectiveness in all 16 KAM360™ drivers.

The distribution of investment priorities underscores three critical aspects of KAM. First, there are no silver bullets. Ultimately, it's a system, and it requires effectiveness in all the drivers to achieve a world-class KAM capability. Second, KAM is a journey. The top investment priorities for any organization are a function of where they are along that journey. No organization can or should address all the drivers at once. Third, KAM is a bridge you're never done painting. Unrelenting continuous improvement is a hallmark of the world's most admired KAM organizations.

"BUSINESS-TO-ECOSYSTEM" IS THE LONGER-TERM TREND

Life sciences' evolution toward more advanced solutions, CEPs, OMs and talent is exciting. Looking somewhat longer-term, we envision other important changes. In particular, we believe life sciences will evolve from business models that approach organized customers, physicians, patients and intermediaries as relatively independent entities to more of an integrated "business-to-ecosystem" (B2E) approach. Intermediaries, in this case, include entities such as pathway companies, pharmacy benefit managers and a host of other players that make up the healthcare system. Third parties, such as high-tech companies and other entities entering the healthcare space, will also become increasingly important constituents and potential partners.

B2E will be a more holistic and integrated approach to engaging the healthcare system, allowing life sciences companies to better address increasing system complexity while boosting organized customer impact. We see three potential implications of the B2E approach for KAM:

1. Advanced solutions and partnerships will incorporate and leverage more nontraditional ecosystem players with capabilities beyond anything life sciences companies could do on their own. We see early signs of this today, for instance, in relation to the trend toward addressing broader social determinants of health. While medical care and genetics account for 30%

of an individual's health, the social determinants of health are responsible for 70% of a patient's overall health—such factors as socioeconomic status, lifestyle, education, access to care, food insecurity and living conditions. To advance health equity, ecosystem customers will need to prioritize addressing gaps in social determinants of health. While life sciences manufacturers are limited in their ability to support this today, there are new companies to partner with to help forge these broader partnerships. This could be as simple as teaming with a ride-sharing service to help patients get the care they need. Or it could be more complex, such as mobilizing with a blockchain-based healthcare platform and an accountable care organization to track and monitor progress and administer easier care and payment coordination for patients.

2. We'll see growth in roles like medical account managers or population health account managers. Because many organized customers increasingly care about creating real-world evidence, supporting phase 4 clinical trials, establishing their own protocols and conducting their own research, the opportunities for life sciences companies to engage are increasingly clinical and medical in nature rather than commercial. Given the regulatory firewalls between medical and commercial teams, particularly in the pharmaceutical industry, roles like medical account managers are becoming more common to help companies address organized customers' noncommercial needs. The trick is ensuring these roles work in tandem with their commercial KAM counterparts as part of the holistic KAM strategy.

3. The B2E approach will require even more advanced customer engagement processes and operating models, as the entire business model shifts to break down organizational silos; drive integration across patient, payer, organized provider, individual hospital and physician functions; and partner with outside organizations with additional capabilities beyond anything that exists in the industry to date.

While these are glimpses into a future state, we believe laying the foundations for world-class KAM today will position companies to successfully address these future changes and capitalize on the opportunities they present.

CONCLUDING THOUGHTS

The evolving prominence, power and priorities of organized customers has been a game-changer for pharmaceutical and medtech companies alike. As many leaders commented during our research, the age-old standard of selling products to clinicians won't be sufficient for success in the emerging environment—especially with increasing organized customer control over individual clinician and hospital practices and product choices.

KAM is a strategic priority in life sciences and will become even more important in the years ahead in lockstep with industry trends in organized customer size, needs, centralized decision-making, control and partnering orientation. A majority of both pharmaceutical and medtech organizations intend to develop advanced solutions beyond basic products to address organized customers' broader needs and priorities. At the same time, many of these same companies will invest in the new engagement processes, operating models, talent and tools necessary to tailor and implement advanced solutions for individual customers. Organizations are at different stages of their journey, and their roadmaps will vary accordingly. Longer-term, KAM strategies will be infused with the more holistic B2E business models that life sciences needs to adopt.

Pharmaceutical and medtech companies can learn a great deal from KAM pioneers and leaders in other industries. But many of the KAM practices employed by outside industries aren't designed for plug-and-play in life sciences. Life sciences' unique customer dynamics and legal considerations require industry-specific value strategies that can impact how key account teams can and should engage with organized customers. It's also important to recognize that pharmaceutical and medtech companies are rapidly contributing to KAM best practices that can be applied outside of life sciences. Next-generation KAM models and approaches are beginning to emerge from within life sciences, and some of them match or exceed the sophistication that generally exists in other industries.

In this book, we have provided a comprehensive framework and leading practices for building world-class KAM strategies and capabilities in life sciences. The central theme has been that life sciences companies must approach KAM as an organization-wide business strategy, not as a role or a sales-only initiative. Per the KAM360™ framework, we have encouraged you to "think system, not silver bullet" and "staged evolution, not one-time event." You should "meet your organization where it is," prioritize and ensure that "form follows function." Together, these principles provide a guiding light for what's sure to be an exciting journey.

NOTES

1 ZS and Strategic Account Management Association, "State of Key Account Management in Pharma" and "State of Key Account Management in Medtech," Q4 2020.
2 Anu Singh et al., "M&A Quarterly Activity Report: Q2 2021," Kaufman Hall, July 8, 2021, https://www.kaufmanhall.com/insights/research-report/ma-quarterly-activity-report-q2-2021.
3 Adam J. Fein, "The Top Pharmacy Benefit Managers of 2020: Vertical Integration Drives Consolidation (rerun)," Drug Channels, June 22, 2021, https://www.drugchannels.net/2021/06/the-top-pharmacy-benefit-managers-of.html.
4 ZS, "Provider Organization Partnership Tracker Wave 3" study, November 2020.
5 ZS, "Provider Organization Partnership Tracker Wave 3" study, November 2020.

6 Alekhya Manne and Shania Sarabhai, "Formulary Exclusion Strategies Promote Cost Savings Amid Pandemic," Clarivate, February 9, 2021, https://clarivate.com/blog/formulary-exclusion-strategies-promote-cost-savings-amid-pandemic/.
7 ZS, "Provider Organization Partnership Tracker Wave 3" study, November 2020.
8 ZS, AccessMonitor: July–December 2020 data period.
9 ZS's March 2021 qualitative research with health system administrators.
10 Net promoter score (NPS) is defined as the fraction of customers rating themselves as promoters (score of 9–10) minus the fraction rating themselves as detractors (score of 0–6) to the question "How likely would you be to recommend [x] to a friend or colleague?" on a 10-point scale, ranging from 0 (not at all likely) to 10 (extremely likely).
11 ZS, "Provider Organization Partnership Tracker Wave 3" study, November 2020.
12 ZS and Strategic Account Management Association, "State of Key Account Management in Pharma" and "State of Key Account Management in Medtech," Q4 2020.
13 ZS and Strategic Account Management Association, "State of Key Account Management in Medtech," Q4 2020.
14 ZS and Strategic Account Management Association, "State of Key Account Management in Pharma" and "State of Key Account Management in Medtech," Q4 2020.
15 Ian Wilcox, Tania Lennon, Bernadette Maher and Jordan Less, "The Future of Selling in Healthcare: An Approach to Disruptive Change," ZS, https://www.zs.com/insights/the-future-of-selling-in-healthcare-an-approach-to-disruptive-change.

ABOUT THE AUTHORS

Mike Moorman is a leading expert in key account management and B2B sales strategy and transformation. He's a principal at ZS and leads the firm's key account management solutions area. Mike founded ZS's B2B commercial strategy and transformation practice and has worked globally with more than 50 organizations spanning 12 industries. He serves on the board of directors for the Strategic Account Management Association and is an adjunct lecturer at the Kellogg Business School Executives Program. Mike is a frequent guest speaker on KAM and sales force topics, has authored more than 60 articles and has been quoted in leading publications, including *Harvard Business Review*, *Financial Times*, *The Wall Street Journal*, *IndustryWeek*, *USA Today* and *Selling Power*. He's based in Chicago.

Rohan Agni specializes in medtech commercial strategy and effectiveness and is a core member of ZS's healthcare ecosystems practice. He focuses on developing leading-edge customer insight, commercial models and capability solutions to maximize medtech and pharmaceutical company impact with health systems and provider groups. Rohan is an associate principal based in Evanston.

Chad Albrecht is a leading expert in incentive compensation design for sales forces and key account management organizations. He's a principal at ZS and leads the sales compensation practice for the medtech industry. Chad leads compensation benchmarking studies for both the Strategic Account Management Association and ZS. Chad has published more than 100 articles and spoken at over 50 conferences on the topic of sales and KAM compensation. He's based in Chicago.

Brian Chapman is a principal at ZS and leads the firm's medtech industry vertical. For nearly 20 years, Brian has worked with global medtech companies on a variety of sales and marketing issues, from portfolio assessment and due diligence to downstream sales force optimization and performance measurement. In the field of key account management, Brian has helped medtech companies design, build and measure KAM capabilities in the United States and around the world. Brian is based in Evanston.

Falko Graf-Meisner is an expert in commercial strategy and customer engagement excellence in life sciences. He brings extensive experience in the design and implementation of global and local key account management programs with a focus on Europe. Falko is an associate principal in ZS's Frankfurt office.

Ankit Jain is a principal at ZS and a leader in the firm's digital and technology practice. He's also a senior member of ZS's healthcare ecosystem practice. Ankit partners with life sciences companies to advise on a broad range of digital technology and analytics transformation issues, including enabling customer engagement strategies in the ever-evolving healthcare ecosystem. He's based in Philadelphia.

Pratap Khedkar is the CEO at ZS. Previously leading the firm's pharmaceutical and biotech industry practice, he has advised life sciences companies on a broad range of commercial strategy and effectiveness issues, with recent work focusing on developing effective strategies and analytics for changing customers in the new healthcare ecosystem. Pratap serves on the board of the Virtua Health System, a $2 billion health system in New Jersey. He's based in Philadelphia.

Jude Konzelmann is a principal at ZS and leads the firm's commercial organization design practice. Jude has extensive experience in both biopharmaceuticals and medtech and brings deep expertise in key account management and in commercial strategy and operations. Jude is a founding principal of ZS's healthcare ecosystem think tank that focuses on future trends and solutions for life sciences. Jude is based in New York.

Tobi Laczkowski is a principal at ZS and works extensively with medtech companies on a broad range of commercial strategy and effectiveness issues, including key account management, go-to-market strategy, sales force effectiveness and compensation plan design. Tobi is an active contributor to ZS thought leadership through a series of published articles and conference engagements and is based in Evanston.

Tania Lennon is a ZS principal based in London and leads ZS's global expertise team focused on enabling organizations to fully capitalize on the potential and performance of their people. Her research and experience include global studies in multigenerational workforce, the future of work and evolving key account management competencies and learning journeys. Tania lectures at the Kellogg Business School Executives Program and was a teaching fellow at the University of London.

Bernadette Maher is a consultant at ZS and a member of the firm's strategy and transformation team, with a specific focus on talent development. Her focus includes leadership development, change management, talent strategy, personnel assessment approaches, sales process design and sales training. Bernadette has a Ph.D. in educational psychology from Temple University. She's based in Philadelphia.

Chris Morgan is a principal at ZS and leads the firm's global talent management practice. He specializes in helping clients overcome the challenges of translating business strategies into local actions through the complexities of cross-functional organizations. He's a frequent guest speaker on key account management at international symposia and U.K. business schools. Chris is based in London.

Mike Powers is a principal at ZS and is a leader in ZS's business consulting practice, where he focuses on commercial strategy, operations and technology. In addition to his client work, Mike helps drive innovation within ZS's key account management technology offerings, including ZS's account planning solutions and partnerships with industry-leading KAM technology platforms. Mike is based in Zurich.

Namita Powers is a principal at ZS and leads the firm's healthcare ecosystem practice, focused on helping life sciences companies design and implement strategies for complex health systems and group practices. Namita is an expert in commercial model strategy, design and effectiveness and has worked extensively with life sciences companies to evaluate and improve key account management program effectiveness. Namita is based in Philadelphia.

Matt Ruple is an expert in life sciences commercial strategy, B2B advanced solutions and value proposition design, go-to-market models, brand marketing and navigating the evolving healthcare ecosystem. He's a principal in ZS's Princeton office and a member of the healthcare ecosystem practice.

Alex Simon is an associate principal at ZS and a member of the key account management solutions team, supporting KAM work across ZS's pharmaceutical and medtech clients. He has supported diverse KAM strategy and capability-building initiatives and specializes in customer engagement process design and account planning and management. Alex is based in Evanston.

Joe Stevens is a leading expert in payer and provider health system needs, buying processes and trends within life sciences. His work focuses on helping life sciences companies develop value strategies and commercial models to engage effectively with payers, large providers and other life sciences organized customers. Joe is a principal in ZS's San Francisco office and is a member of the value and access and the healthcare ecosystem practices.

Subhashri (Shubha) Suresh is an expert on key account management incentives and MBO design in life sciences. Shubha has extensive experience in pharma and biotech, focusing on KAM and sales force incentives design and implementation. She's a principal in ZS's San Francisco office.

ACKNOWLEDGMENTS

Editing and co-authoring a book in partnership with 16 of the leading experts in their respective fields has been an incredible journey and privilege. I am greatly indebted to all the authors, whose names appear at the start of each chapter and whose photographs and biographies are provided in the "About the authors" section. The authors are all members of ZS, a global management consulting firm, whose more than 10,000 associates help many of the world's leading organizations with everything from product innovation to commercialization—including the strategy, analytics and technology to achieve impact where it matters.

The co-authors have each tapped into a wealth of personal KAM experience specific to their area of expertise to collectively address all aspects of KAM in life sciences. Despite the many challenges and demands the authors face in their roles at ZS, they have put forth tremendous effort and shown great patience in writing this book. They spent countless hours collaborating with me and each other, sharing their wisdom and responding to my all-too-often unrealistic requests and deadlines.

In addition, many other colleagues at ZS have contributed to the book. Elizabeth Torp was a tireless project manager, helping us organize and orchestrate every aspect of the process while also personally providing final editorial review. Andrew Dolbeare and Rebecca Knutsen provided insightful editorial advice to our co-authors throughout the process. Nidhi Chauhan designed the book's cover. She, along with several other graphic designers, including Varun Roy, Indraneel Guha and Rick Shipman, also developed the figures used throughout the book. Lastly, Kelly Urkov and Andrea Moore assisted not only with project management throughout, but also with content and book promotions.

I would also like to thank the ZS partners, including Bernie Thiel and Angela Hummel at Alterra Group, who provided comprehensive editorial reviews and manuscript development; and our publishing partner Routledge, including Rebecca Marsh and her exceptional team.

Without the efforts of these talented and hardworking collaborators, this ambitious book would not have come to life.

Mike Moorman

INDEX

Note: **Bold** page numbers refer to tables; *italic* page numbers refer to figures and page numbers followed by "n" denote endnotes.